Big Book of
Crystal Beads

First Published in North America in 2008 by
CREATIVE HOMEOWNER®
Upper Saddle River, NJ 07458

CRE▲TIVE
HOMEOWNER®

Creative Homeowner® is a registered trademark of Federal Marketing Corporation.

Originally published as *Le Grand Livre des Perles de Cristal*
© GROUPE FLEURUS, November 2005
15/27, rue Moussorgski
75895 Paris cedex 18

The author thanks the Bouveret fabric shop for its support.

The editor thanks PERLES BOX, who graciously supplied all of the beads and materials used in creating the jewelry, and Aventures Creatives.

Editorial Direction: Christophe Savouré
Editors: Christine Hooghe and Anne Garnier
Art Direction: Laurent Quellet and Thérèse Jauze
Production: Thierry Dubus and Catherine Maestrati
Design and Execution: Vanessa Blondel and Sabrina Regoui
Photography: Patrice Renard
Illustrations: Catherine Hélye-Lebaron

To my mother, Monique, for her support and to my aunt Marie-France, whom I miss very much.

CREATIVE HOMEOWNER

SENIOR EDITOR: Carol Endler Sterbenz
DESIGNER: Maureen Mulligan
EDITORIAL ASSISTANTS: Nora Grace and Jennifer Calvert
TECHNICAL EDITOR: Emily Harste
TRANSLATOR: Janice Clark

VP/PUBLISHER: Timothy O. Bakke
PRODUCTION DIRECTOR: Kimberly H. Vivas
ART DIRECTOR: David Geer
MANAGING EDITOR: Fran J. Donegan

ISBN-10: 1-58011-385-0
ISBN-13: 978-1-58011-385-4

CREATIVE HOMEOWNER®
A Division of Federal Marketing Corp.
24 Park Way
Upper Saddle River, NJ 07458
www.creativehomeowner.com

Big Book of Crystal Beads

PATRICIA PONCE

CREATIVE HOMEOWNER®, Upper Saddle River, New Jersey

TABLE OF CONTENTS

Introduction

Little compares to the shimmer and sparkle of crystal beads, and in this lavishly illustrated volume, over 70 pieces of beautiful jewelry made using crystal beads are presented in a collection suited to every season and occasion.

Now, you will be able to create rings, necklaces, pendants, chokers, bracelets, and pins made from crystals in unique combinations of dazzling color—from a pendant in ruby red and earrings in whisper pink and blue to a bracelet in the palest yellow. Each original design is shown in detailed, full-color photographs and precise, easy-to-follow, color-coded diagrams that lead you from stringing on the first light-catching crystal to tying off the threads of your beautiful creation.

To further help you make each must-have piece, there is an introductory section about the basic tools and materials that you will need and a comprehensive tutorial on the basic techniques to make all the designs in the book. In addition, the skill level of each beaded project is indicated. It is important to read these sections before you begin if you are not used to working with crystal beads and threading bead assemblies.

BEADS

Crystal Beads

◆ Bicones

These sparkling crystal beads are available in a broad range of colors. The 4mm bicone comes in more than 180 colors and in matte, glossy, or iridescent finishes. Sizes range from 3mm to 10mm. Most of the designs in this book are made using 4mm and 6mm bicones.

◆ Shapes

Crystal beads come in many shapes, such as:
- flowers (6mm, 8mm, 10mm)
- cubes (4mm, 6mm, 8mm)
- bicones (6mm x 15mm)
- hearts (10mm x 10mm–50mm x 50mm)
- faceted open-cut squares (14mm, 20mm, 30mm)
- faceted round balls (3mm–10mm dia.)
- buttons (12mm diameter faceted shallow cones with a hole drilled through the center of the back)

Note: Other round beads that can be used are faceted glass or faux pearls

◆ Mounted jewels

Mounted (or montée) jewels are crystal, glass, or acrylic gemstone shapes set in copper, gold, or silver settings that have stringing holes in the base. The shapes can be emerald, square, oval, marquise, etc., and are available

Montée Jewels

in many sizes. Mounted jewels add a touch of sophistication to rings as well as pendants.

◆ Rhinestone rondelles

These small "wheels" of gold, copper, or silver metal are set with tiny rhinestones and are available in many colors. From 5mm to 8mm in diameter, they can beautify a pendant clasp or accentuate the sparkle of a ring.

◆ Rhinestone balls

These beads are made of flat-back rhinestones mounted on a hollow metal bead. They come in many colors and range in size from 4.5mm to 10mm in diameter.

Rhinestone balls and rhinestone rondelles

Bicones

Hearts and flowers

Faceted oval and round
beads, and a bicone (center)

Other beads

◆ Rocailles

These tiny beads are ofen referred to as seed beads, but they have a slightly different shape — they are less squat. They are usually lined in silver and measure approximately 1mm to 3mm in diameter. There is an extensive color range and finishes can be matte, metallized, iridescent, or lustrous.

Size 11/0 rocailles are crucial in the assembly of most of the designs in this book. They fill gaps between other beads and conceal the stringing threads. Choose a color that matches or contrasts with the other bead colors used in the design. When in doubt, refer to the materials list or use clear rocailles.

Delicas are recommended because they are perfectly uniform and symmetrical. They are more expensive than other rocailles, but are essential for even weaving.

◆ Faceted ovals

These slightly oval-shaped glass beads are available in sizes from 3mm to 8mm in diameter and larger. They are also available in a broad range of colors and finishes. Faceted ovals are used in this book for weaving bases and most ring bands.

Roses

◆ Roses

Metal roses in gold, silver, and metallic colors enhance the appearance of beaded jewelry. The beading hole for metal roses is located in the center of the rose, from top to bottom. By delicately manipulating the petals you can recreate the look of real roses. Choose carefully because some of these roses chip easily. To prevent chipping, always coat the petals with clear nail polish before using.

Rocailles

Faceted ovals

HELPFUL TIPS

◆ Crystal beads are unique because their color changes subtly in different types of light. When new, they have a bright sparkle but they will lose that shine and become dull from handling. To restore the brightness of their shine, polish them gently with a soft cloth.

◆ Hard water can easily dull the brilliance of crystal beads. To preserve their clarity, avoid getting them wet.

FINDINGS

These are the metal accessories in silver, gold, or copper that are used to connect design elements and complete the designs. To prevent an allergic reaction, do not use findings with a nickel content.

Findings

Clasp

Bead tips

These findings are available in a variety of sizes and shapes, and are used to hide thread knots at the ends of bracelet and necklace strands. They are also used to join several strands; clasps or jump rings are then attached to the bead tips.

Bead tip

There are two types of bead tips:

- **Those that close vertically.** Insert the thread through the bottom hole; knot it several times; then gently close the bead tip using flat-nose pliers.
- **Those that close horizontally.** Knot the thread end; insert the knot into the bead tip; and close it using flat-nose pliers.

Always apply a little dab of glue or clear nail polish to the knot. Allow the glue to dry; trim the thread end close to the knot; then close the bead tip.

To reinforce a very small knot, string on a rocaille bead, placing it at the base of the knot. Enclose both the rocaille and the knot in the bead tip. When finished, attach a clasp or jump ring, as needed, to the bead tip.

End caps

End caps finish the ends of ribbons or cords used for pendant necklaces. They are available in gold, silver, and copper.

- **If ribbon is used,** make a knot at each end and trim the ribbon end close to the knot. Place the knots in the end caps, and use flat-nose pliers to squeeze the cap edges so that they overlap and close.
- **If cord is used,** knot the cord ends and then follow the directions for ribbon on page 14.

Clasps

Clasps are used to fasten bracelets and necklaces. They are available in many shapes and in metallic colors that coordinate with different beads and styles of jewelry. For many designers, the choice of a clasp is important to the success of a piece. The simplest clasps are spring-ring and barrel clasps. Barrel clasps should not be used for bracelets because they are difficult to secure using one hand. Also used are lobster-claw clasps, multi-strand clasps, magnetic clasps, and adjustable clasps

Jump rings

Jump rings are used to secure the clasp to the design. They can be purchased or made using eye or headpins and round-nose pliers. To open a jump ring without distorting it, place pliers on either side of the opening. Bring one end of the ring toward you and the other away from you. Close the jump ring in the same way. To avoid scratches, apply masking tape to the tips of both pairs of pliers.

Eye pins and headpins

These are wires that are available in various lengths. An eye pin has a ring at one end, and a headpin has a flat, nail-like head. In this book they are used for drop earrings and for making jump rings.

Earrings

Findings are manufactured in many different styles and metals for both pierced and clip-on earrings.

The earring designs in this book are made using hook-style ear wires and ear studs for pierced ears. The same designs can be easily adapted for use with non-pierced earring findings.

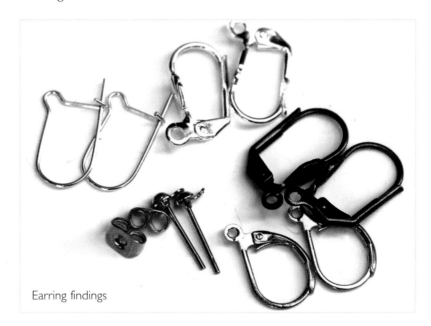

Earring findings

End caps

Lobster-claw clasp

Pin backs

These findings come in sizes ranging from ¾ in. (19mm) to 1½ in. (38mm) long. The bar of the pin is pierced with two to three holes to which assembled beads are attached.

Ring mounts

There are two parts to a ring mount:
- ◆ A disk backing welded to an adjustable ring
- ◆ A pierced disk on which the beads are secured

The pierced disk is secured to the mount by using flat-nose pliers to bend down metal tabs on the disk backing. Ring mounts come in several sizes and metal colors.

Disk backing and ring

Pierced disk

Assembled ring mount

STRANDS

Ribbons and cords

Ribbons can be made from fabrics such as velvet, chiffon, lace, or satin. They can also be made from woven metallic thread. Cords are usually made of satin, but silk cord is available as well. Choose what you like best to personalize your jewelry. Be careful when choosing metallic ribbons; some are stretchy and can lose their shape.

Beading thread

C-Thru Thread is an almost clear, woven thread that knots well. The majority of the examples in this book are made with a fine J-weight thread. This thread is able to pass through a bead several times.

Use K-weight thread for rings that require only a few passes of thread through each bead. Also, use K-weight for bracelets, necklaces, and simple pendants.

Wire

Gold, silver, or color-plated wires used in jewelry-making are rigid but sufficiently bendable to obtain and retain the desired shape. When working with wire, avoid getting kinks, which can weaken the wire, causing it to break.

Cable wire

Cable wire is available in a broad palette of colors. It is manufactured from a twisted stainless-steel wire core that is coated with nylon. Ideal for simple bead stringing, this material is flexible and strong. Lightweight cable is 0.014 in. (0.4mm) in diameter.

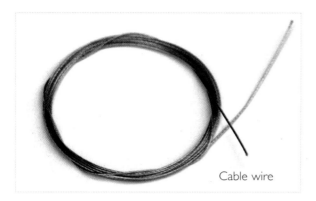

Cable wire

NEEDLES

Flexible beading needles make stringing beads with beading thread easy. Use a needle at each end when working with both ends of a strand of beading thread. Use a beading needle that has a large eye that collapses when going through beads. If your needle is too long and unweildly, trim it shorter using wire cutters.

Needle threader

Use a needle threader when you are not able to insert a threaded needle through a bead. Lightly flatten the wire tip of the threader with your fingers, and insert it into the bead hole. Insert the thread into the tip, and pull at the base of the threader to pull the thread through the bead.

Straight pins and needles

Straight pins and sewing needles can be used to open knots. They are also used to clear a bead hole for easy threading. Never force a pin or needle through the beading hole; the pin can break off or damage the bead.

TOOLS

Flat-nose pliers

Flat-nose pliers are indispensable when making bracelets, necklaces, and pendants. They serve several functions:
- To secure metallic end caps to ribbons or cords
- To close bead tips
- To open and close jump rings
- To flatten crimp beads

They are also necessary when attaching findings to ribbons and cords for pendants.

Round-nose pliers

Use these pliers to form wire into rounded shapes, such as when making a loop or forming jump rings from eye pins and headpins.

Wire cutters

Use wire cutters to cut wire and beading thread.

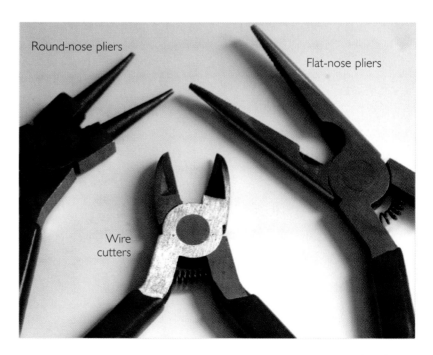

Round-nose pliers

Flat-nose pliers

Wire cutters

BASIC TECHNIQUES

BEFORE YOU START

The diagrams and photos, as well as the list of materials that accompanies each design, will help you distinguish the different shapes, sizes, and colors of beads used in a project. Lay out the beads needed to make the design following the diagram. A handy work surface is a large jar lid or a small tray with a rim. Glue felt into the bottom to keep the beads contained and so that they do not roll around. Felt glued to the underside of the lid will provide a non-slip surface for the container.

ASSEMBLING THE DESIGN

Thread the needles, and begin assembling the beads following the diagram. Unless indicated, always string the first beads onto the center of the thread. After the first two steps, be sure that the thread ends are identical in length, or you will not be able to correctly finish the piece. Stop after each step to check that you haven't made a mistake, such as forgetting to thread on a bead or reversing colors, which would mean that you would have to begin again.

LEVEL OF DIFFICULTY

The difficulty of each assembly is indicated by 1 to 3 stars:

VERY EASY ★ ☆ ☆

EASY ★ ★ ☆

DIFFICULT ★ ★ ★

FOLLOWING A DIAGRAM

A green arrow indicates the starting point of the assembly. Carefully read the directions that accompany the diagrams before beginning.

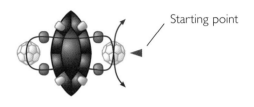

Starting point

A diagram accompanies each step of the directions. Beads added in the step are shown in color: gray beads indicate where threads pass through the beads strung in a previous step; white beads indicate the position of the beads strung in previous steps but *not* used in the current step. One thread end is red and the other is blue. Arrows indicate the weaving direction and the ends of the threads. Dashed lines indicate the threads brought from one side of the work to the other.

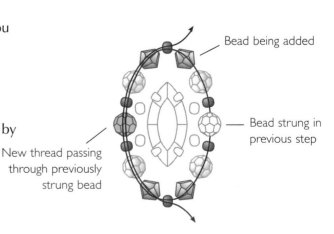

Bead being added

Bead strung in previous step

New thread passing through previously strung bead

PLACING CERTAIN BEADS HORIZONTALLY

Flat beads, such as flowers, rondelles, and metallic roses, are held in place with one rocaille.

Pass both thread ends through the bottom of the flat bead, and thread one rocaille onto both thread ends. Pass the thread ends back into the same hole in the flat bead, and pull tight.

Example: Nosegay Pendant,
Diagram 3 (See page 36.)

ASSEMBLING PICKS

Picks are "stems" of beads made in various lengths according to the design. The beads are framed by one rocaille placed at each end. First, thread on the beads necessary for the creation of the pick. Finish each end with one rocaille; then pass the thread back through the beads in the same sequence. It is important to keep the thread tight so that the pick is straight. To do this, gently pull the thread ends while holding the rocaille between your fingers.

Example: Enchanted Bracelet, Diagram 3
(See page 126.) A double pick
around one bicone

RINGS

Making a ring band

A ring band is made by extending the setting of the ring using the same threads. Band size is determined by the number of beads used. The bead pattern for a band must begin and end with the same-style beads so that the pattern is symmetrical. The choice of band design and the size of the beads used is up to you. For example, begin a band by stringing one 4mm bicone of the same color on each thread end. Then cross the threads through one 4mm bicone of a different color. To work the band pattern, string two rocailles on each thread. Then cross the threads through one 4mm faceted oval of the same color. Repeat this pattern to the desired length. (Be sure to include the ending beads when sizing the ring.) End the same way you began. Cross the threads through one bicone, and add one bicone of the same color on each thread. (See "Finishing a Ring Band," on page 19.) A few variations on the ring band are possible:

- Variation 1: Add only one rocaille between a 4mm faceted oval.

Example: Knight's
Ring
Diagram 3
(See page 144.)

- Variation 2: Use 3mm faceted ovals and two rocailles.

Example: Planet Ring
Diagram 7
(See page 160.)

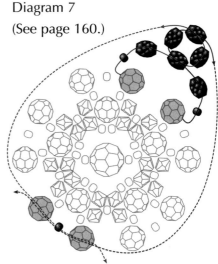

- Variation 3: Create a band using only rocailles, crossing the threads in a minimum of two rocailles. Make the band long enough so that it's comfortable.

Example: Infinity Ring
Diagram 5
(See page 168.)

Finishing a ring band

When you have reached the desired band length, hold the thread ends tight in one hand, and smooth the beads toward the setting with your other hand to tighten the band. Cross the threads in the identical bead on the other side of the setting. Reinforce the ring by passing both threads once more through all the beads of the ring. End by passing the threads together so that they join. Knot the threads as described below, and trim the ends.

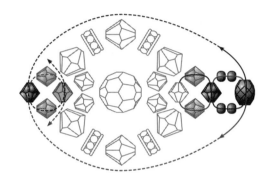

Example: Du Barry Ring
Diagram 3 (See page 44.)

Choosing bead color for a ring band

Use beads in the band that echo the main color of the ring setting. However, it is not always possible to find faceted ovals that exactly match the color used in the setting. In that case, use a colorless bead.

Sizing a ring band

The materials list for each ring specifies 12 faceted ovals for an average-size ring band and identifies the color used for the sample ring. Depending on the ring size desired, fewer or more beads may be needed.

PENDANT LOOPS

If a pendant is to lie flat, the hanging cord or ribbon must go through the beaded loop so that it is parallel with the pendant. The beaded loop is made in an "X" shape. The end of each leg of the X is secured to the pendant top, and the cord or ribbon is threaded through the legs.

ENDING THE THREADS

Once the design is assembled, pass both thread ends through the beads so that they join and exit the same bead hole. Working on the wrong side, make three knots, one on top of the other as follows: make a simple knot; then cross the threads, and knot them in the opposite direction; and finally, make a simple knot.

To hide the thread ends, pass them through an adjoining bead; then pull them so that the knots slide into the bead hole. Trim to 1 in. (25mm), and insert the ends into adjacent beads.

When a design has a mounted jewel in the center, bring the thread ends to the back of the jewel to knot them. Apply glue or clear nail polish to the knots, and let it dry. Trim the thread ends to 1 in. (25mm), and insert them into adjacent beads.

THE CROSS TECHNIQUES

The cross technique is used in the assembly of all the designs. It consists of crossing two threads in the same bead so that they exit on opposite sides of the bead (Diagram 1). When using this technique, hold the bead in which the threads cross each other in your fingers.

THE SQUARE CROSS

This technique consists of stringing three beads onto one thread and crossing the ends through a fourth bead to form a square. To increase the size of the square, place one rocaille between each bead (Diagram 2).

As shown in diagrams 3, 4, and 5, different forms can be made by assembling several squares.

Making a row or column

The first square consists of four beads, with the threads crossing in the fourth bead. Then, string three beads to form the next square, and cross through the third bead (Diagram 3).

Making a square*
(* with the same number of vertical and horizontal rows)

Assemble the first row of two squares, and end by crossing the threads in the bottom bead. To do this, string three beads on the outside thread, and cross through the bottom bead.

For the third square (bottom right), string three beads on the outside thread, and cross through the left bead.

For the fourth square (bottom left), add two beads. (The other two were strung during the assembly of the preceding squares.) Pass the inside thread through the bottom bead of the preceding row. Add two beads to this thread. Cross the threads through the bottom left bead. This assembly is also called a carpet (Diagram 4).

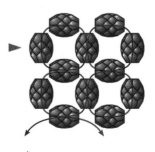

Making a rectangle

Follow the same directions as for the square, but with an uneven number of rows and columns.

Making a cross

The third (top) and fourth (bottom) squares in this shape are assembled using a single thread. Do this by placing four beads on the thread; then cross through the first bead. When assembling a square, it is essential to tighten the work well (Diagram 5).

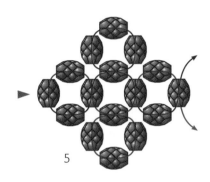

5

THE FLOWER

Flowers are woven on an assembly of bead squares.

The classic flower

Flowers are usually made with four bicones and one rocaille. The bicones represent the petals, and the rocaille represents the center of the flower.

Each flower is worked on a base of bead squares. First, make a square using four faceted oval beads (Diagram 2). String one bicone on each thread. Cross the threads in one rocaille, and string a bicone on each thread. To secure the flower to the square, cross the threads in the opposite faceted oval of the square (Diagram 6).

Tighten the threads. See Diagram 7 for the finished design.

Other types of flowers

There are other flower designs. To make the design in Diagram 8, string one rocaille on each thread; cross them in one 6mm bicone; then string one rocaille on each thread again. The bicone is positioned horizontally on the square. To have the bicone vertical, string one rocaille on each thread; pass the threads together through the bicone; then string one rocaille on each thread (Diagram 9).

If you wish to use this method with a 4mm bicone, thread two rocailles on each side to compensate for the smaller size of the bicone.

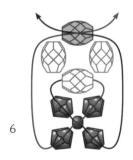

6

7

8

9

THE ROSE TECHNIQUE

The rose techinique consists of assembling beads into triangles and assembling beaded triangles side by side, which then form a circle. There are several assembly possibilities, but the basic technique is always the same. Beads of different shapes and sizes may be used. To familiarize yourself with assembling roses, begin with "The 4-Rose."

THE 4-ROSE

As its name suggests, "The 4-Rose" shape consists of four triangles. The following example is made using eight 4mm light and dark bicones.

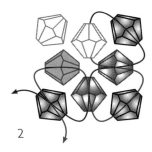

Center one light bicone, one dark bicone, and one light bicone on the thread. Cross the other end of the thread in the first bead. The first triangle is complete when the threads cross in the bead on the right (Diagram 1).

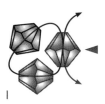

For the second triangle, on the outside thread, string one dark bicone and one light bicone. Cross the inside thread in this last bead (Diagram 2).

Make the third triangle in the same way as shown.

For the fourth triangle, insert the inside thread through the light bicone at the starting point. Add one dark bicone, and cross the outside thread in this last bicone.

The four dark bicones will be on the outside, and the four light bicones will be on the inside. (See the "Butterfly Ring," on page 54.)

THE 5-ROSE

"The 5-Rose" shape consists of five triangles using ten 4mm bicones and rocailles.

Center one light bicone, one rocaille, one light bicone, one rocaille, one dark bicone, and one rocaille on the thread. Cross through the first bicone to complete the first triangle (Diagram 3).

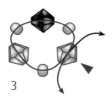

Assemble the second triangle by adding one rocaille, one dark bicone, one rocaille, and one light bicone on the outside thread. Add one rocaille on the inside thread; then cross the inside thread in the light bicone.

Repeat this process twice more for triangles 3 and 4.

String one rocaille and one dark bicone on the outside thread (Diagram 4). String one rocaille on the inside thread. Pass the inside thread through the light bicone at the starting point. Add one rocaille; then cross the inside thread in the dark bicone. (See "Emerald Earrings," page 94.)

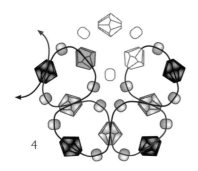

When you count the beads for the assembly of "The 5-Rose" shown in Diagram 4, there should be:

- ◆ Five rocailles in the center
- ◆ Five light bicones on the inside
- ◆ Five dark bicones on the outside, each with one rocaille on either side.

THE 6-ROSE

"The 6-Rose" is made of six triangles. The following example is made using six 6mm faceted ovals, six rocailles, and six 4mm bicones in colors 1 and 2.

On the thread, center one bicone in color 1, one faceted oval, one bicone in color 2, and one rocaille. Then cross through the first bicone. The first triangle is completed (Diagram 5).

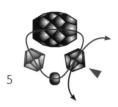

5

Assemble the next four triangles following Diagram 6. String one faceted oval on the outside thread. String one rocaille on the inside thread. Cross the threads through one bicone in color 1 or color 2. For the sixth triangle, add one rocaille to the inside thread; then pass it through the first bicone. Cross the threads in one faceted oval. (See the " Lucky Turtle Pendant," on page 74.)

THE 8-ROSE

The method of assembly for "The 8-Rose" is identical to the previous rose but with eight triangles. (See the "Indian Summer Pendant," on page 116.)

COVERED ROSES

First make a 4-, 5-, 6-, or 8-rose as shown in the examples described. This assembly will be used as a base or "carpet" into which the other beads are worked. (See the "Ocean Ring," on page 166.)

ANOTHER ROSE ASSEMBLY

This technique consists of first assembling the outside band of the rose. Then triangles are assembled above the band.

For "The 6-Rose," string six 4mm faceted ovals on the thread, and cross them through the first faceted oval. Add one bicone, one rocaille, and one bicone to the blue thread. Cross the red thread in the last bicone. Pass the blue thread through the next faceted oval (Diagram 7).

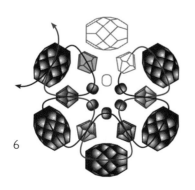

6

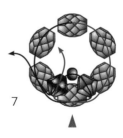

7

To assemble the second triangle, thread one rocaille and one bicone on the red thread. Cross the blue thread in this last bicone.

Pass the red thread through the next faceted oval to begin the next triangle (Diagram 8). Repeat three times.

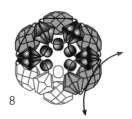

To assemble the sixth triangle, string one rocaille on the inside thread. Pass the thread through the first bicone strung; then cross the threads in the faceted oval below.

HELPFUL TIPS

- The best way to avoid mistakes is to check your work at each step by counting the beads.

- Pull the threads tight at each step of the assembly so that the design is even and firm. To avoid breaking the threads, always pull them close to the beads.

- If you make a mistake and have to restring part of the assembly, take the design apart carefully. Bead hole edges can be sharp (especially bicones), so be sure not to abrade the threads when you remove the beads or you will weaken them.

Spring

To celebrate the return of sun-and-
breeze-filled days, create unique pieces of
crystal jewelry in the colors of Spring—pale
pink, sky blue, and opalescent mauve. Enjoy the
sparkle of "Rose Bed" on your wrist; indulge
your fantasies with the "Starlet Set." Let the
wings of the "Butterfly" ring grace your
finger. A burst of fresh color like flowers that
bloom under the first rays of sun, each
crystal creation appears to be woven from
beads of morning dew.

Materials

1 round decorative glass bead, 8mm dia., color A (pink)

10 bicones, 4mm dia., color A (pink)

4 bicones, 6mm dia., color B (green)

10 cat's eyes round beads, 4mm dia., color C (pale green)

11/0 rocailles, pink

12 faceted ovals, crystal (for ring band)

52 in. (1.3m) beading thread
2 beading needles

Difficulty ★ ★ ★

TRANSLUCENT RING

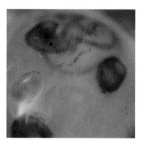

1 On the thread, center three 4mm bicones in color A. Then cross through one 6mm bicone in color B. On each thread, string one rocaille, one cat's eye, one rocaille, one 6mm bicone in color B, one rocaille, one cat's eye, and one rocaille. Then cross them in one 6mm bicone. On the left thread, string three 4mm bicones, and pass them back through the last 6mm bicone.

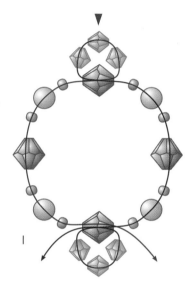

2 On each thread, string three rocailles. Pass both threads through the round bead. String three more rocailles on each thread, and cross through the first 6mm bicone.

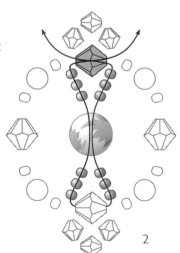

TIP
To make this piece with more classic style, replace the cat's eyes and the round beads with crystal beads.

3

Pass both threads to the 6mm bicones on the left and right. On the right thread (blue), add one rocaille, one cat's eye, and one rocaille. Cross in the round bead. String one rocaille, one cat's eye, and one rocaille. Cross through the 6mm bicone on the left. Repeat for the left thread (red).

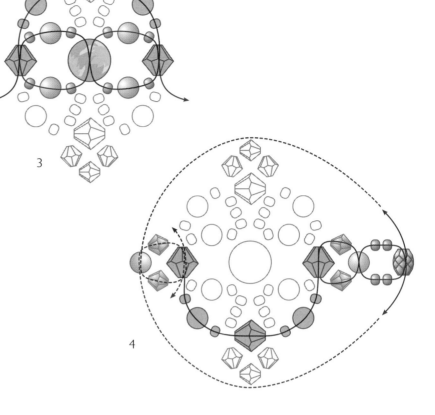

3

4

Pass the left thread through the 6mm bicone on the right. Refer to page 18 to begin the ring band, using two 4mm bicones in color A. Cross through one cat's eye. Continue the ring band with the rocailles and faceted ovals. Finish the band with one cat's eye and two bicones in color A. Join the thread, and make a knot.

4

MAUREEN RING

Materials

24 bicones, 4mm dia., color A (pink)

1 marquise montée, 15mm long, color B (fuchsia)

10 bicones, 4mm dia., color B (fuchsia)

18 round beads, 4mm dia., color C (crystal)

11/0 rocailles, rose

12 faceted ovals, rose (for ring band)

52 in. (1.3m) beading thread

2 beading needles

Difficulty ★ ★ ★

1 On the center of the thread, string one round and one rocaille. Pass through the top holes of the monteé. String one rocaille, one round bead, and one rocaille. Pass through the bottom holes of the montée. String one rocaille, and cross through the first round bead.

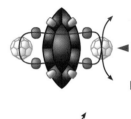

2 On each thread, string one rocaille, one round bead, one bicone in color A, one rocaille, one bicone in color A, one round bead, and one rocaille. Cross in the opposite round bead; then pass each thread through the four succeeding beads.

3 On the top thread, string one bicone in color B, two rocailles, one bicone in color A, two rocailles, and one bicone in color B. Pass back through the first rocaille. Repeat with bottom thread.

4 Pass each thread again in the last bicone strung. Add one round bead, one bicone in color A, and one round bead. Cross the threads in one bicone in color B on the right.

5 On each thread, string one rocaille, and one bicone in color A. Cross in the top and bottom holes of the montée. On each thread, string one bicone in color A and one rocaille. Cross in one bicone in color B on the left. On the bottom thread (red), add one round bead, one bicone in color A, and one round bead. Pass through two rocailles and the bottom bicone. Repeat with the top thread (blue). Pass through two rocailles on the top left, the top bicone, and all beads on the right. Cross in the bottom bicone.

6 Pass the threads back through the rocailles. Pass through two bicones; cross through one rocaille; and pass through two bicones. String one round bead on each thread; cross in a montée; and string one round bead on each thread. Pass through two bicones; cross through one rocaille; and pass through two bicones.

7 On each thread, add one bicone in color A, one round bead, two bicones in color A, one round bead, and one bicone in color A. Pass two rocailles; cross one bicone; and pass through two rocailles. Pass the left thread to cross the center bicone on the left. Pass the right thread through the beads on the outside, and cross the center bicone

on the left. Refer to page 18 to begin the ring band with two bicones in color B and one bicone in color A. Add rocailles and faceted ovals for the band. End symmetrically. Join the threads, and knot them.

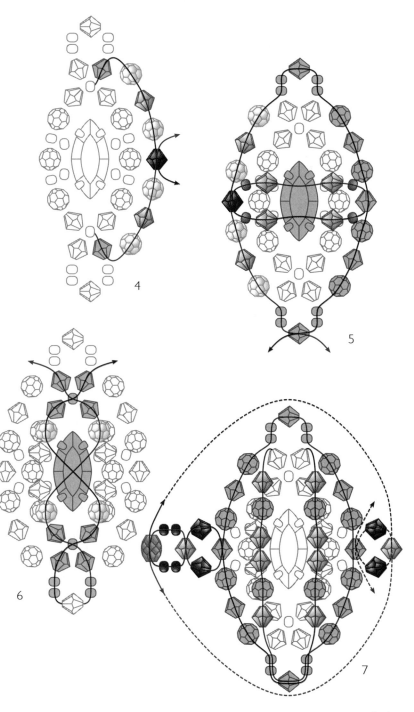

STARLET SET

Earrings materials

14 bicones, 4mm dia., color A (fuchsia)

8 bicones, 4mm dia., color B (mauve)

2 rhinestone balls, 8mm dia., color C (crystal)

11/0 rocailles, mauve

Hook ear wires, silver

2 strands 16 in. (40.6 cm) beading thread

2 beading needles

Diffficulty ★ ★ ★

Technique: Assembling Picks (See page 17.)

Earrings

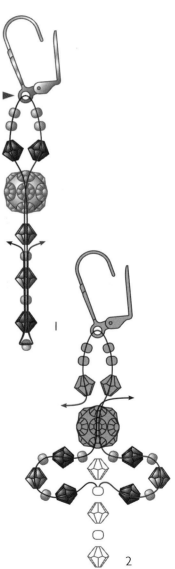

1 | Make two earrings. Center the loop of the ear wire on the thread. On each end of the thread, string two rocailles and one bicone in color A. Pass the threads through one rhinestone ball, one bicone in color B, one rocaille, one bicone incolor B, one rocaille, one bicone in color A, and one rocaille. Cross into the bottom bicone and three succeeding beads to create a pick.

2 | On each thread, place one bicone in color A, one rocaille, one bicone in color B, one rocaille, one bicone in color A, and one rocaille. Cross the thread through the rhinestone ball. Pass the right thread through six top beads, and join with the left thread. Knot the threads.

TIP
You can lengthen the pick by stringing on more bicones and by adding beads when making the horizontal loops.

Ring

1 | Center one 6mm bicone in color A on the thread. On each end, string one rhinestone rondelle, three 6mm bicones, alternating colors, and one rhinestone rondelle. Cross through one 6mm bicone in color A.

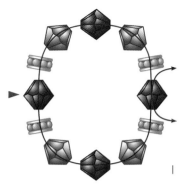

2 | Add one 4mm bicone in color B on each end. Cross through the rhinestone ball. Add one 4mm bicone in color B on each end. Cross the threads in the left bicone.

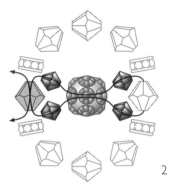

3 | Pass the top thread (red) to the top bicone. Add one rocaille, one 4mm bicone in color A, and one rocaille. Cross in the rhinestone ball, and add the same series of beads again. Pass through the bottom bicone.

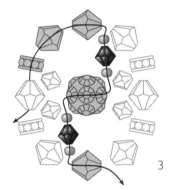

4 | Pass the bottom thread (blue) from the left bicone to the bottom bicone. Add one rocaille, one 4mm bicone in color A, and one rocaille. Cross in the rhinestone ball. Add the same series of beads again. Pass through the top bicone and the beads on the right to cross in the right bicone. Pass the bottom thread (red) through the beads on the right to cross in the right bicone. Refer to page 18, beginning the band with the bicones. Continue with the rocailles and faceted ovals. Finish symmetrically. Join the threads; then knot them.

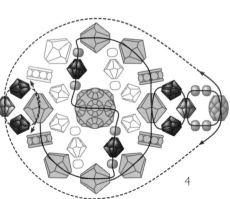

Ring materials

4 bicones, 6mm dia., color A (fuchsia)

8 bicones, 4mm dia., color A (fuchsia)

4 bicones, 6mm dia., color B (mauve)

6 bicones, 4mm dia., color B (mauve)

4 rhinestone rondelles, 5mm dia., color C (crystal)

1 rhinestone ball, 8mm, color C (crystal)

11/0 rocailles, mauve

12 faceted ovals, fuchsia (for ring band)

52 in. (1.3m) beading thread

2 beading needles

Difficulty ★ ★ ★

TIP
To add even more sparkle to the design, choose an iridescent finish for one of the bead colors.

STARLET SET

Pendant

1 | Center one rocaille, one 6mm bicone in color A, and one rocaille on each thread. On each end, add one rhinestone ball; then cross through one 6mm bicone in color B. Add one rhinestone ball on each end. Cross through one 4mm bicone in color A. String one 4mm bicone in color B on each end. Pass both through one rhinestone ball, one 4mm bicone in color A, and one rocaille. Pass both threads to the first 4mm bicone in color A that was strung. Cross through that bicone. Tighten the threads symmetrically so that the pick is straight.

2 | On each thread, string one rocaille, one 4mm bicone in color B, one rocaille, one 6mm bicone in color A, one rocaille, one 6mm bicone in color B, one rocaille, and one 4mm bicone in color A. Cross in the center 6mm bicone. Pass each end through a rhinestone ball. Add one rocaille on each thread; then cross in the top 6mm bicone.

3 | For the loop, add two 4mm bicones of different colors on each end. Cross through an additional 4mm bicone. String six rocailles on each end. Cross again through top 6mm bicone. Pass through a few beads to join the threads; then knot.

Pendant materials

3 bicones, 6 mm dia., color A (fuchsia)

6 bicones, 4 mm dia., color A (fuchsia)

3 bicones, 6mm dia., color B (mauve)

7 bicones, 4mm dia., color B (mauve)

5 rhinestone balls 8mm dia. in color C (crystal)

11/0 rocailles in mauve

Hanging ribbon or cord with findings as desired

52 in. (1.3m) beading thread

2 beading needles

Difficulty ★ ★ ★

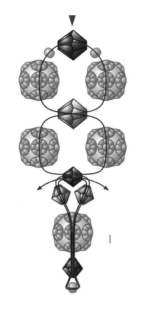

1

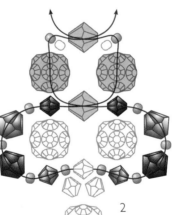

2

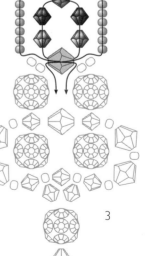

3

NOSEGAY PENDANT

Materials

4 faceted ovals, 4mm dia., color A (violet)

8 bicones, 6mm dia., color A (violet)

8 bicones, 6mm dia., color B (mauve)

7 bicones, 4mm dia., color C (peach)

16 faceted ovals, 6mm dia., color C (peach)

1 metal rose, 10mm dia., color B (mauve)

11/0 rocailles, peach

Hanging ribbon or cord with findings as desired

40 in. (1.0m) beading thread

2 beading needles

Difficulty ★ ★ ☆

Technique: The Square Cross (See page 20.)

1 Make the first square using four 6mm faceted ovals. On the right thread, string one 4mm faceted oval and four 6mm faceted ovals. Cross in the first 6mm bead to make a second square. Add one 4mm faceted oval. Repeat with the left thread to make a third square. Cross in one 6mm faceted oval. Make the last square using three 6mm faceted ovals.

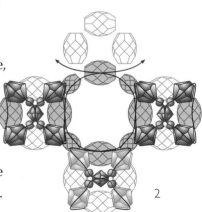

2 For the first flower, on each end have one 6mm bicone in color A and one rocaille. Cross in one 4mm bicone. Add one rocaille and one 6mm bicone in color A on each end. Cross the oval at the top of the square. Pass the right end to cross in the left oval of the second square. Add one 6mm bicone in color B, one rocaille, one 4mm bicone, one rocaille, and one 6mm bicone in color B. Cross through the right oval. Add one 6mm bicone in color B and one rocaille. Cross through the 4mm bicone. Add one rocaille and one 6mm bicone in color B. Cross through the left oval of the square. Pass to cross through the bottom oval of

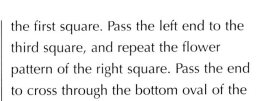

the first square. Pass the left end to the third square, and repeat the flower pattern of the right square. Pass the end to cross through the bottom oval of the first square.

3 Pass both threads through the metal rose from the underside. Pass through one rocaille and back through the rose. Cross in the opposite faceted oval. Pass each thread to cross in the faceted oval at the bottom of the pendant.

4 Turn the assembly over, and pass each thread around the pendant, inserting one rocaille between each 6mm faceted oval. Cross the threads in the top faceted oval of the first square.

5 Make the fourth flower by repeating the directions for the first flower in step 2. Cross in the bottom faceted oval of the first square. Pass the right thread through the next two faceted ovals.

6 Pass the left thread through the left and top faceted ovals of the first square. On each thread, string one 4mm bicone in color C and five rocailles. Cross them in a 4mm bicone. Thread five more rocailles on each thread. Pass each end through the bottom 4mm bicones. Pass the ends through the beads to meet at the back, and make a knot.

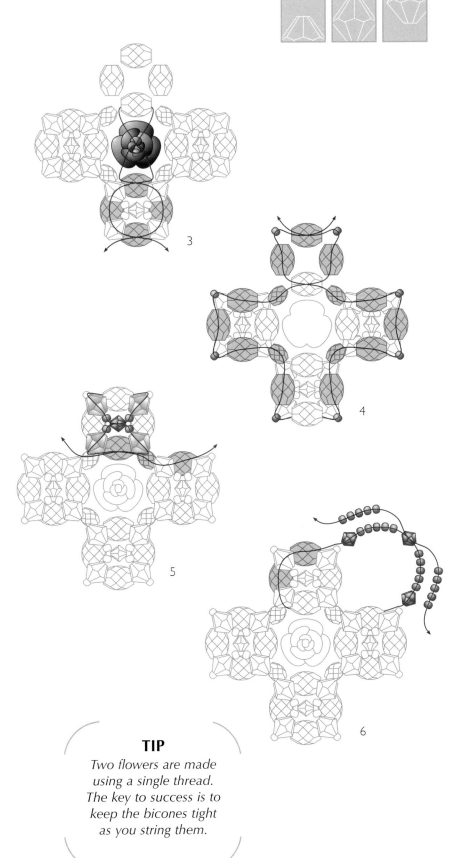

TIP

Two flowers are made using a single thread. The key to success is to keep the bicones tight as you string them.

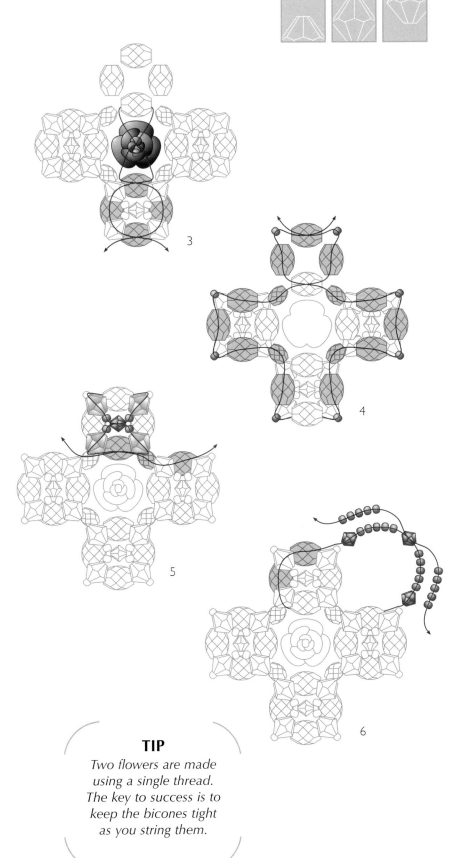

MORNING-GLORY RING

Material

2 hearts, 10mm x 10mm, color A (violet)

2 hearts, 10mm x 10mm, color B (pink)

8 bicones, 4mm dia., color A (violet)

8 bicones, 4mm dia., color B (rose)

11/0 rocailles, pink

1 ring mount and beading disk with 19 holes

52 in. (1.3m) beading thread

2 beading needles

Difficulty

1. Have the rounded surface of the disk face up. Insert the thread end from the back of the disk into an outside hole and through the back of one heart in color A. String one rocaille, and pass back through the heart and the same hole. The thread ends are on the back of the disk.

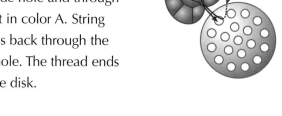

1

2. Insert the second thread from the back through the nearest hole toward the center of the disk. Insert it into the heart and through the first hole to the back. The thread ends are on the back of the disk.

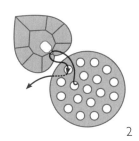

2

3. Skip two holes to the left, and bring the left thread to the front of the disk. String one heart in color B and one rocaille as in steps 1 and 2. Skip two holes to the left, and repeat, stringing one heart in color A and one rocaille. Skip two holes to the right, and bring the right thread to the front of the disk. String one heart in color B and one rocaille. Bring the threads to front of the disk as shown by the arrows.

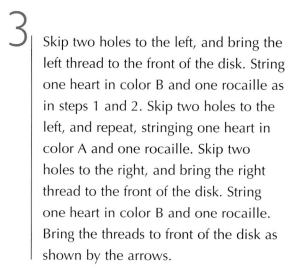

3

4

On the right thread (blue), string alternating colors of four bicones. Pass the thread to the back of the disk where shown. (The bicones form an arch.) Bring the thread to the front of the disk where shown, and string two bicones in alternating colors and one rocaille. Pass back through two bicones and the disk to make a pick. On the left thread (red), string two bicones in alternating colors and one rocaille to make a pick. Pass back through the same hole.

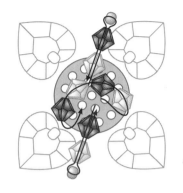

TIP
The difficulty of this piece stems from keeping the threads tight at each step. To achieve this, hold onto the threads through all steps.

5

Pass one thread to the front of the disk through a hole between two hearts. Make a pick with two bicones in alternating colors and one rocaille. Pass back through the same hole. Repeat around the disk, stringing three more picks between the hearts. Pass both threads together to the back, and make a knot. Apply glue, and cut the threads. Place the disk on the mount, and use flat-nose pliers to secure it with the tabs on the mount.

Materials

6 faceted ovals, 4mm dia., color A (peach)

18 bicones, 4mm dia., color A (peach)

10 bicones, 4mm dia., color B (crystal)

1 round bead 8mm dia. in color B (crystal)

8 bicones, 4mm dia., color C (pale peach)

11/0 rocailles, peach

12 faceted ovals, peach (for ring band)

52 in. (1.3m) beading thread

2 beading needles

Difficulty ★ ★ ★

Technique: The 6-Rose (See page 24.)

PEONY RING

1 Center one bicone in color C, one faceted oval, and two rocailles on the thread. Working to the right, cross the threads through one faceted oval. On the inside thread, add two rocailles. On the outside thread, add one bicone in color C. Cross in one faceted oval. Repeat three more times. Add two rocailles on the inside thread, and pass the ends as shown.

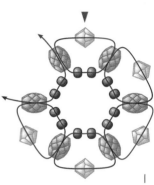

2 Bring the threads together, and pass through a round bead. Separate the threads, and pass them through two faceted ovals opposite them. Pass each thread through two rocailles and the following faceted oval. Hold the threads tight, and position the round bead in the center.

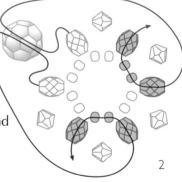

3 Pass the top thread (red) through the bicone at the left. Add one rocaille, one bicone in color C, and one rocaille. Pass through one bicone; add one rocaille; and pass through one bicone. Pass the bottom thread (blue) to the right. Add one rocaille between each pair of bicones that do not have one. Cross the threads as shown.

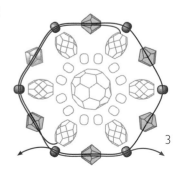

4 On the left thread, string one bicone in color A, one bicone in color B, and one bicone in color A. Pass through the beginning rocaille. Pass through the bicone and the following rocaille. Thread two bicones in color B and one bicone in color A. Pass back through the rocaille. Repeat once more, reversing the colors. See the diagram for the right thread and bicone colors, and where to cross the threads in one bicone in color B. Pay attention to color placement.

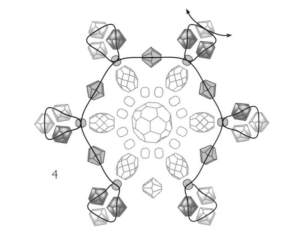

5 On the left thread and working toward the left, add one rocaille, one bicone in color A, and one rocaille. Pass through the following bicone. Continue around the outside, and cross through the beginning bicone. Pass the right thread toward the right, through all outside beads, and cross through the beginning bicone.

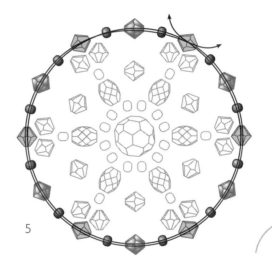

6 Pass the threads toward the center of the assembly, as shown, so they cross through the two rocailles closest to the round bead. Refer to page 18 to begin the ring band at this round bead. String one bicone in color A on each thread, and cross through one bicone in color C. String two rocailles on each thread, and cross in one faceted oval. Repeat rocaille and faceted oval pattern. End the band symmetrically with one bicone in color C and two bicones in color A. Cross the threads in the rocailles opposite the ones from the beginning. Join the threads, and make a knot.

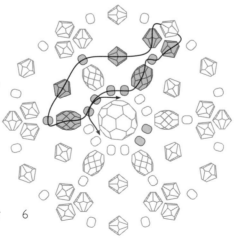

TIP
Beginning in step 5, you will notice that the round bead and the four bicones in color B are strung on the same horizontal line. To get a perfect finish, it is important to have the ring band extend from this line.

Materials

4 faceted ovals, 6mm dia., color A (crystal)

16 bicones, 4mm dia., color B (opalescent mauve)

9 bicones, 4mm dia., color C (mauve)

1 round montée, 4mm dia., color C (mauve)

11/0 rocailles, purple

Hanging ribbon or cord with findings as desired

40 in. (1m) beading thread

2 beading needles

Difficulty ★ ★ ★

Technique: The Square Cross (See page 20.)

FORGET-ME-NOT PENDANT

1 | Make a square of four faceted ovals. On each thread, string one rocaille and one bicone in color B. Cross through the montée. On each thread, string one bicone in color B and one rocaille. Cross in the top faceted oval.

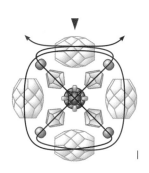

2 | On the right thread, add three bicones in color B. Pass back through the oval. Add one bicone in color C, and pass through the following oval. Add three bicones in color B, and pass through the oval. Add one bicone in color C, and cross the bottom oval. On the left thread, add one bicone in color C, and pass through the following oval. Add three bicones in color B, and pass through the oval. Add one bicone in color C, and cross the bottom oval. Add three bicones in color B, and pass through the oval.

TIP

For this design, choose a color for the rocaille that is bolder than that of the bicones.

3 Follow the diagram, and string four flowers using the rocailles and bicones in color C. Have the threads cross in the top bicone.

4 For the loop, string four rocailles on each thread. Cross through one bicone in color C. String four rocailles on each thread. Cross through the top bicone of the flower. Pass through a few beads to join the threads; then make a knot.

3

4

Materials

4 bicones, 6mm dia., color A (blue)

2 bicones, 4mm dia., color A (blue)

4 rhinestone rondelles, 5mm dia., color A (blue)

2 bicones, 6mm dia., color B (gray blue)

2 bicones, 4mm dia., color B (gray blue)

8 bicones, 4mm dia., color C (opalescent blue)

1 round bead, 8mm dia., color D (crystal)

11/0 rocailles, blue

12 faceted ovals in crystal (for ring band)

52 in. (1.3m) beading thread

2 beading needles

Difficulty ★ ★ ★

DU BARRY RING

I At the center of the thread, place one 4mm bicone in color B. On each side, add one 6mm bicone in color A, one rhinestone rondelle, one 6mm bicone in color B, one rhinestone rondelle, and one 6mm bicone in color A. Cross through one 4mm bicone in color B.

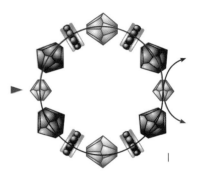

2 On each thread, add one 4mm bicone in color C. Cross the threads through a round bead. On each thread, add one 4mm bicone in color C. Cross through the bicone on the left. Pass each thread through the outside beads, and cross through the bicone on the right.

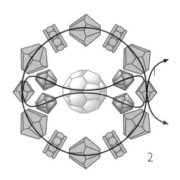

3 On each thread, have two 4mm bicones in color C. Cross through one 4mm bicone in color A. Refer to page 18 to begin the ring band, adding two rocailles on each thread, and crossing in one faceted oval. Finish the band symmetrically. Join the threads, and make a knot.

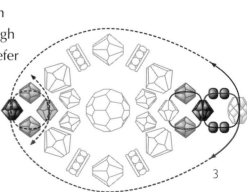

Pendant materials

24 faceted ovals, 4mm dia., color A (violet)

16 bicones, 4mm dia., color B (mauve)

1 bicone, 6mm dia., color B (mauve)

13 bicones, 4mm dia., color C (dark purple)

6 bicones, 4mm dia., color D (opalescent violet)

11/0 rocailles, violet

Hanging ribbon or cord with findings as desired

40 in. (1m) beading thread

2 beading needless

Difficulty ★ ★ ☆

Technique: The Square Cross (See page 20.)

VEGA SET

Pendant

1 Make a square with four faceted ovals. Cross in the top faceted oval. For the flower, on each end have one 4mm bicone in color C. Cross in one rocaille. Add one 4mm bicone in color B on each end, and cross in the bottom faceted oval.

2 On the right thread, string one rocaille and four faceted ovals. For the pattern, pass back through the first oval strung, and add one rocaille. Repeat once. Repeat twice with the left thread. Cross through one faceted oval. On each thread, string one faceted oval. Cross through a fourth faceted oval to complete the bottom square. Follow step one for the flower. Have color C on the outside and color B on the inside. Cross inside the faceted oval.

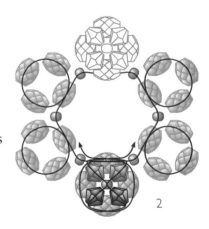

TIP
Carefully observe the placement of the flower colors. Color C is always on the outside, and color B is always on the inside of the pendant.

3 Pass each thread to the bottom of the next square. Using one thread at each square, string the flowers by passing through the center rocaille and the faceted ovals. Pass through the top two rocailles.

4 String two rocailles on each thread. Cross in a 6mm bicone, and add two rocailles to each thread. Following the diagram, cross through the top faceted oval of the bottom square. Pass each thread through the side ovals, and cross in the bottom faceted oval.

5 On the left thread and working left, add two rocailles, one 4mm bicone in color D, and two rocailles. Pass through the following oval. Repeat twice. Cross through the oval at the top. Repeat with the right thread. Add two 4mm bicones in color C on each thread. Cross through one 4mm bicone in color B. Add six rocailles on each thread. Cross the threads through the top oval. Pass the threads through the beads to join them; then make a knot.

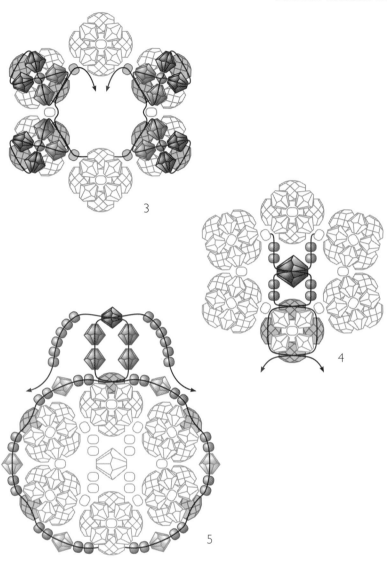

Earring Materials

40 faceted ovals, 4mm dia., color A (violet)

20 bicones, 4mm dia., color B (mauve)

20 bicones 4mm dia., color C (dark purple)

11/0 rocailles, violet

Hook ear wires, silver

2 strands, 32 in. (80cm), beading thread

2 beading needles

Difficutly

Technique: The Square Cross (See page 20.)

VEGA SET

Earrings

Make two earrings. Repeat steps 1–3 of the pendant on pages 46 and 47, making five squares. Have color B bicones on the outside and color C bicones on the inside. Cross the threads in the top oval. Add one rocaille on the right thread. At the right, pass through the right oval of the square, the rocaille at the bottom, and the left oval of the second square. Add one rocaille. Pass through the top oval of the second square. Repeat around. Cross through the top oval of the first square. String three rocailles on each thread. Cross through the loop of the ear wire. Pass back through the rocailles. Pass through several beads to join them before knotting.

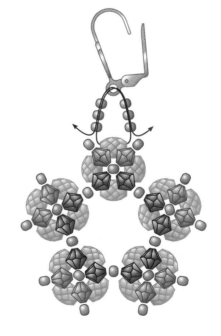

Materials

1 heart, 10mm x 10mm, color A (mauve)

5 bicones, 4mm dia., color A (mauve)

1 heart, 30mm x 30mm, color B (pink)

12 bicones, 4mm dia., color B (pink)

11/0 rocailles, pink

Hanging ribbon or cord with findings as desired

40-in. (1.0m) length of 24-gauge wire in gold

Difficulty ★ ★ ★

Technique: Assembling Picks (See page 17.)

DOUBLE-HEART PENDANT

1 Thread two bicones in color B on the center of the wire. Cross the 30mm x 30mm heart. The wire in front should be 6 in. (15cm) or longer.

2 On the wire at the back of the heart, string five bicones following the diagram for the hanging loop. Pass the wire from the front of the heart to the back. Pass it once again through the same bicones and through the hole in the heart to the back.

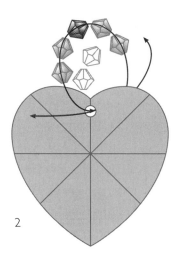

TIP
Because the wire is somewhat fine, it kinks easily. Avoid this, as kinks can weaken the wire and cause it to break.

3 On the front wire, string the 10mm x 10mm heart. Add one rocaille, five bicones (alternating the colors), and one rocaille. To make the first pick, pass the wire back through the bicones and the center rocaille. Repeat to make the second pick. Pass the wire through both hearts, and exit at the back. Pass both wire ends through the hanging loop and back through the hole of the 30mm x 30mm heart. Trim the ends short enough to be concealed behind the 10mm x 10mm heart.

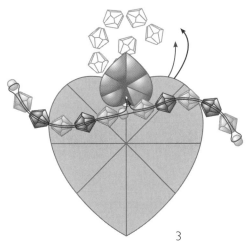

3

CLEMATIS RING

Materials

2 bicones, 6mm dia., color A (pale pink)

8 bicones, 4mm dia., color A (pale pink)

4 bicones, 6mm dia., color B (purple)

2 bicones, 4mm dia., color B (purple)

4 bicones, 4mm dia., color C (pink)

5 rhinestone rondelles, 5mm dia., color D (crystal)

11/0 rocailles, pink

12 faceted ovals, pink (for ring band)

52 in. (1.3m) beading thread

2 beading needles

Difficulty ★ ★ ★

1 | Center one 6mm bicone in color B on the thread. On each thread end, string one 4mm bicone in color A, one rhinestone rondelle, one 6mm bicone in color B, one rhinestone rondelle, and one 4mm bicone in color A. Cross through one 6mm bicone in color B.

2 | On each thread, string three rocailles. Pass through one 6mm bicone in color A, one rhinestone rondelle, and one 6mm bicone. Add three rocailles on each thread. Cross through the 6mm bicone.

TIP
To easily pass through the center rhinestone rondelle, thread both thread ends onto one beading needle.

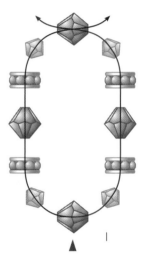

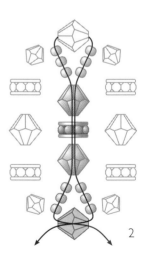

3 Refer to the diagram, and pass each thread through the outside beads. Add one 4mm bicone in color C on each thread. Cross in the center rhinestone rondelle. Add one 4mm bicone in color C on each thread. Pass through the outside beads. Cross in the top 6mm bicone.

4 Pass both threads through the outside beads so that they cross through the right 6mm bicone. Pass each through the rhinestone rondelles.

5 Refer to page 18 to begin the band, placing one 4mm bicone in color A on each thread. Cross through one 4mm bicone in color B. Continue the band with the rocailles and faceted ovals. Finish symmetrically. Join the threads, and make a knot.

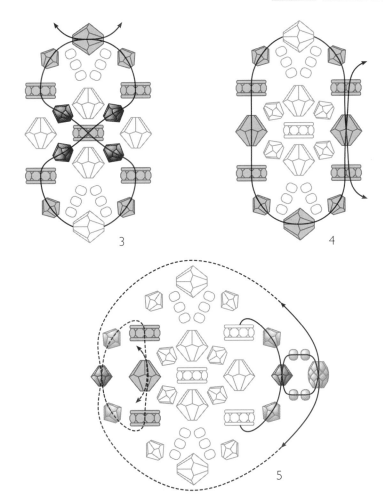

BUTTERFLY RING

Materials

22 bicones, 4mm dia., color A (peach)

6 bicones, 4mm dia., color B (light brown)

8 bicones, 4mm dia., color C (gold)

11/0 rocailles, peach

12 faceted ovals, peach (for ring band)

6 in. (15.2cm) length 24 gauge wire, gold

56 in. (1.4m) beading thread

2 beading needles

Difficulty ★ ★ ★

Techniques: The 4-Rose (See page 22.) Assembling Picks (See page 17.)

1 Make one "4-Rose" with bicones in color A in the middle and bicones in color B on the outside.

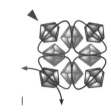

2 On the top thread (red), string one bicone in color C, one rocaille, one bicone in color A, one rocaille, one bicone in color B, one rocaille, one bicone in color A, one rocaille, and one bicone in color C. Pass through the next bicone. Cross through the bicone in color C. Pass the bottom thread (blue) through the next bicone. Add one bicone in color A. Cross through the bicone in color C.

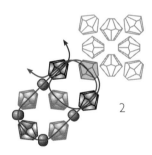

3 String two rocailles on the right thread (blue). Pass through the top left bicone of the rose. Add one bicone in color C, one bicone in color A, and one bicone in color C. Cross through the same bicone of the rose. On the left thread (red), string one rocaille, one bicone in color A, and one rocaille. Cross through the bicone in color A. Make one pick as shown. Cross through the bicone in color C.

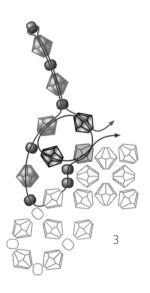

4

Pass both ends through two rocailles. Pass the bottom thread (red) through the top right bicone of the rose. Add two rocailles, one bicone in color C, one rocaille, one bicone in color A, and one bicone in color C. Pass through two rocailles and the bottom right bicone of the rose. On the top thread (blue), string one bicone in color C. Make the pick as in step 3. Add one bicone in color A and one rocaille. Pass through the bicone in color A, one rocaille, and the bicone in color C. Cross through the bottom right bicone of the rose.

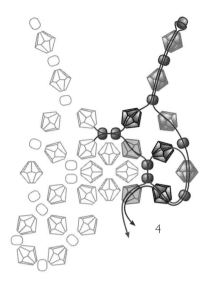

5

On one thread (blue), string one bicone in color C, one rocaille, one bicone in color A, one rocaille, one bicone in color B, one rocaille, one bicone in color A, and one rocaille. Pass through the bicone in color C and the bottom right bicone of the rose. Pass through two rocailles and the bottom left bicone of the rose. Cross through two center left rocailles of the rose. Pass the other thread (red) through the bicone in color C. Add one bicone in color A. Pass though the bicone in color C. Pass through the outside of the rose to cross through two center left rocailles of the rose. Turn the assembly over. Place two bicones in color A on each thread. Cross through one faceted oval. Continue the band with the rocailles and faceted ovals. Finish symmetrically. Join the threads, and make a knot.

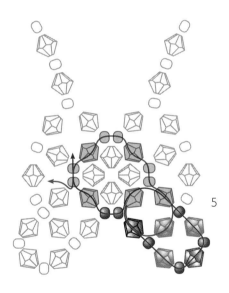

TIP

Pass the short lengths of wire through the wing tips to reinforce them and keep them from bending. Trim the wire ends so that they are centered inside the bicones.

ROSE-GARDEN BRACELET

Materials

70 faceted oval beads, 4mm dia.,
color A (pink)

40 bicones, 4mm dia., color A (pink)

20 bicones, 4mm dia., color B
(dark pink)

20 bicones, 4mm dia., color D
(violet)

2 metal roses, 6mm dia., silver

1 metal rose, 10mm dia., silver

2 bead tips, 2 jump rings, and 1
lobster-claw clasp, silver

11/0 rocailles, pink

2 strands beading thread, each
50 in. (1.3m)

2 beading needles

Difficulty ★ ★ ★

*Techniques: Bead Tips (See page
12.) Clasps (See page 13.)
Jump Rings (See page 13.)
The Square Cross (See page 20.)*

1 Secure both thread ends in one bead
tip. Secure the jump ring and clasp.
String three rocailles on each thread.
Cross through one faceted oval. Make
23 faceted oval squares.

2 Thread nine bicone flowers as shown.
Have color A on one diagonal, and
alternate the two other colors on the
other diagonal. On both threads, string
one 6mm rose from the bottom, and
add one rocaille. Pass back through the
rose. String one flower, one 10mm rose,
one flower, and one 6mm rose. Thread
the nine remaining flowers. Cross in the
last faceted oval.

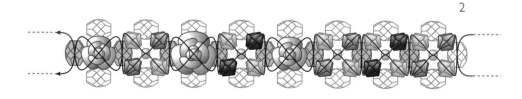

3 Pass each thread through all of the outside faceted ovals to the unfinished end, adding one rocaille between each oval. Cross through the last faceted oval. String three rocailles on each thread, Secure both thread ends in the bead tip. Attach the jump ring.

TIP

In step 3, be sure to pull both threads using the same tension so that the finished bracelet does not curl back on itself.

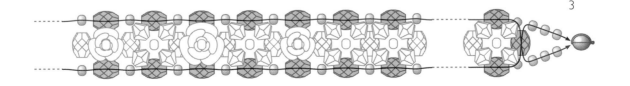

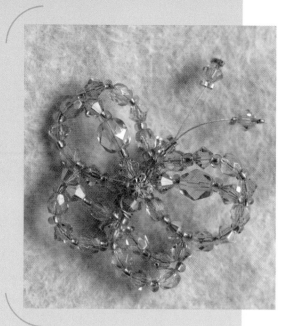

BUTTERFLY PIN

  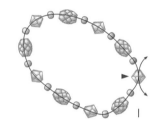

Materials

24 bicones 4mm dia., color A (peach)

16 faceted ovals, 4mm dia., color B (beige)

2 faceted ovals, 6mm dia., color C (sky blue)

1 round montée, 4mm dia., color C (sky blue)

11/0 rocailles, blue

5 crimp tubes, 2mm x 2mm, silver

Crimping pliers

1 pin back, ¾ in. (19.1mm) long, with 2 holes, silver

52-in. (1.3m) length 0.014 in. (0.4mm) cable wire, silver

2 lengths 24-gauge wire, each 4 in. (10cm), silver

Difficulty ★ ★ ★

1 On the wire, center one bicone, one rocaille, one 4mm faceted oval, and one rocaille. Repeat four times, and cross through the first bicone.

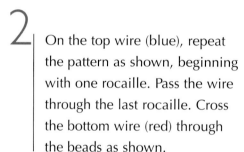

2 On the top wire (blue), repeat the pattern as shown, beginning with one rocaille. Pass the wire through the last rocaille. Cross the bottom wire (red) through the beads as shown.

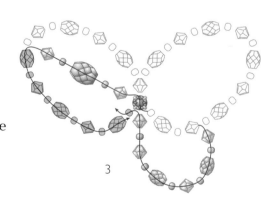

3 On the right wire, add a montée, one bicone, one rocaille, one 4mm faceted oval, one rocaille, one bicone, one rocaille, one 4mm faceted oval, one rocaille, one bicone, one rocaille, and one bicone. Pass through the rocaille at the left. On the left wire, add one bicone, one rocaille, one 6mm faceted oval, one rocaille, and one bicone. Pass through the beads as shown.

4 Pass the left wire (blue) through the rocaille and the montée. Add one bicone, one rocaille, one 6mm faceted oval, one rocaille, and one bicone. Pass through the right side of the wing. Pass the other wire (red) through the beads of the left wing. Add one bicone, one rocaille, one faceted oval, one rocaille, one bicone, one rocaille, one faceted oval, and one rocaille. Pass through the bicone as shown.

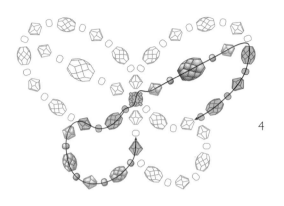

5 On the left wire (red), add one rocaille, one 4mm faceted oval, one rocaille, and one bicone. Pass through the beads to the top of the butterfly. Pass the right wire (blue) through the bicone as shown. Add one bicone, one rocaille, one 4mm faceted oval, and one rocaille. Pass through the beads to top of the butterfly.

6 To begin the antennas, hold the wires together and add one bicone and one crimp tube. Flatten the crimp tube close to the bicone. Separate the wires. On each, flatten a crimp tube ½ in. (12.7mm) from the first crimp tube. Add to each wire one bicone and one crimp tube. Flatten the last crimp tubes, and trim the wires. Secure the butterfly to the pin back with two lengths of gold wire. Wrap the wires where shown by the dashed lines on the diagram. Trim the wires, and tuck the ends under the butterfly.

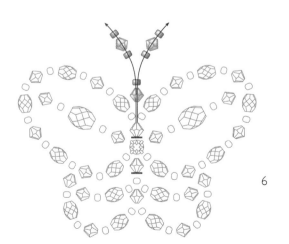

TIP

Flatten the crimp tubes so that they are secure on the wire, but do not use so much force that they become distorted.

Materials

21 bicones, 4mm, color A
(dark green)

39 faceted ovals, 4mm dia., color
B (emerald green)

1 faceted oval, 6mm dia., color C
(crystal)

1 rhinestone rondelle, 6mm dia.,
color C (crystal)

9 flowers, 6mm dia., color C
(crystal)

11/0 rocailles, crystal

Hanging ribbon or cord with findings as desired

80 in. (2m) beading thread

2 beading needles

Difficulty ★ ★ ★

*Techniques: Assembling Picks
(See page 17.) The Square
Cross (See page 20.)*

FLORAL-HEART PENDANT

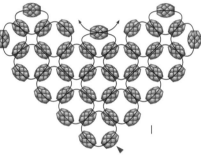

1. Begin at the bottom, and work left to string four faceted oval squares using 4mm beads. Make two triangles of faceted ovals at the top left. Work down to string four squares to the bottom right. Make two more squares up the right side, then two triangles at the top right. Make two more squares going back toward the left. Finish by passing the left thread back through the closest faceted oval. Then cross threads through the last faceted oval.

2. Pass both threads through the back of one flower and one rocaille. Pass back through the flower. Separate the threads, and pass them through the faceted ovals around the heart, adding the bicones and rocailles as shown. At the bottom, pass the right thread through one bicone, one rocaille, and back through the same bicone to complete the pick. Cross the threads in the first faceted oval at left.

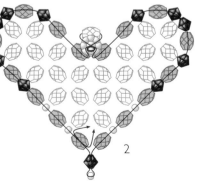

3 Thread one flower and one rocaille onto the first square at the right as in step 2. Cross through the top right faceted oval of the first square. Cross through one bicone. Cross through the top right faceted oval of the second square. Repeat the pattern up the right side, alternating the flowers with bicones. At the corner, cross through the left faceted oval as shown. Cross through one bicone. Pass the top thread (blue) through the top faceted oval. Pass the bottom thread (red) through the bottom faceted oval.

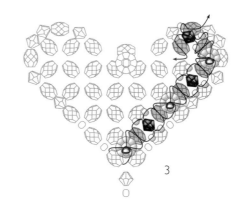

4 Cross the top thread (blue) through the same faceted oval as the red thread. Repeat the pattern to the bottom left, crossing in the last faceted oval of the row.

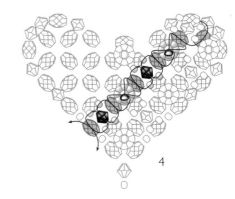

5 Pass the left thread (blue) to the next faceted oval. Pass the right thread through the faceted ovals as shown. Repeat the pattern of one flower and one bicone. Pass the threads as shown to the next row of squares at left. Work one flower and one bicone over each square. Pass the threads as shown.

6 Work one flower and one bicone over each square. Pass the threads as shown to the center. Cross through the top faceted oval. Add one rocaille to each thread. For the hanging loop, pass both threads through one bicone, one rhinestone rondelle, and a 6mm faceted oval. On each thread, add four rocailles. Cross through one bicone. Add four rocailles to each thread. Pass the threads back through a 6mm faceted oval, a rhinestone rondelle, and a bicone. Pass through a few beads on the back; then make a knot.

Summer

With the sun at its brightest, the landscape plays up its richest colors in a season of casual style. Revive the look of your wardrobe with original jewelry designs that show off summer's colors. Encircle your finger with the sophisticated "Moonlight" ring or wear the shimmering "Emerald" earrings. The brilliant colors of all the pieces in this season will flatter and intrigue you, from the first rays of morning sun to the midnight blue of a star-filled sky.

Ring materials

4 cubes, 6mm, color A (crystal)

3 cubes, 4mm, color A (crystal)

2 bicones, 4mm dia., color A (crystal)

10 bicones, 4mm dia., color B (yellow)

11/0 rocailles, yellow

12 faceted ovals, yellow (for ring band)

48 in. (1.2m) beading thread

2 beading needles

Difficulty ★ ★ ★

TIP
*Complete the band
the same way that you
began it. Cross the threads
through one bicone in
color A; then add the last
two bicones in color B.*

SUNSHINE SET

Rings

1 On the thread, center one 4mm cube, two rocailles, two 6mm cubes, two rocailles, one 4mm cube, two rocailles, two 6mm cubes, and two rocailles. Cross the threads in the first 4mm cube.

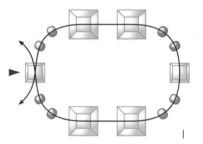

2 On each thread, add three rocailles. Pass both threads through one bicone in color B, one 4mm cube, and one bicone in color B. Add three rocailles on each thread. Cross in a 4mm cube.

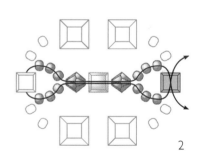

3 Pass the bottom thread (blue) through two rocailles and a 6mm cube. String one bicone in color B. Cross through the center cube. String one bicone in color B. Pass through a 6mm cube and two rocailles. Cross in a 4mm cube. Repeat with the top thread (red).

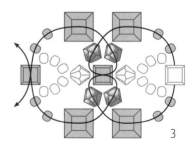

4 On each thread, string one bicone in color B. Cross through one bicone in color A. Continue the ring band with the rocailles and faceted ovals. End symmetrically. Join the threads, and make a knot. (See page 18 for details.)

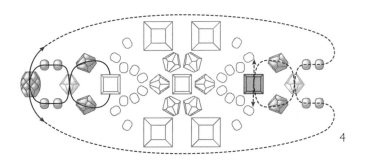

4

SUNSHINE SET

Earring materials

14 bicones, 4mm dia., color A (crystal)

2 cubes, 4mm, color A (crystal)

20 bicones, 4mm dia., color B (yellow)

11/0 rocailles, yellow

Hook ear wires, gold

2 strands beading thread, each 12 in. (30.5cm)

2 beading needles

Difficulty ★ ★ ★

Earrings

1 Make two earrings. Center one bicone in color A on the thread. On each end, add one bicone in color B. Cross in the cube. On each end, add one bicone in color B. Cross in one bicone in color A.

2 On each thread end, string one bicone in color B, two bicones in color A, and one bicone in color B. Cross in one bicone. On each end, add three rocailles. Pass both ends through one bicone.

3 Cross in the loop of the ear wire. Add one bicone in color B to each end. Bring the ends around the back of the ear wire as shown.

4 Pass each end through one bicone in color B. Add one rocaille to each end. Pass the ends through one bicone. Pass each through the rocailles. Cross in one bicone. Pass each through a bicone; then pass them together through a cube. Knot the threads.

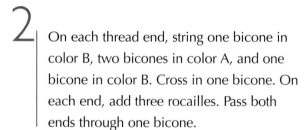

TIP

When tightening, use the same tension on each thread end to avoid a lopsided earring.

DAHLIA RING

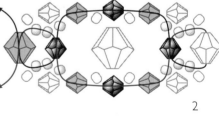

Materials

2 bicones, 6mm dia., color A
(deep blue)

14 bicones, 4mm dia., color A
(deep blue)

16 bicones, 4mm dia., color B
(sky blue)

1 bicone, 8mm dia., color C
(crystal)

11/0 rocailles, crystal

12 faceted ovals, sky blue
(for ring band)

52 in. (1.3m) beading thread

2 beading needles

Difficulty ★ ★ ★

I | Center one 6mm bicone on the thread. On each end, add one rocaille, two 4mm bicones in color B, and one rocaille. Cross through the 8mm bicone. Repeat and cross one 6mm bicone as shown.

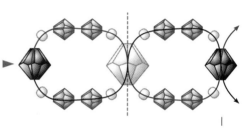

2 | On each thread end, add two rocailles. Cross through one 4mm bicone in color A. Add one rocaille to each thread. Pass through the second 4mm bicone from step one. Add one 4mm bicone in color A. Pass through the next 4mm bicone from step 1. Add one rocaille, and cross in one 4mm bicone in color A. Add two rocailles to each thread, and cross in a 6mm bicone.

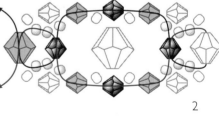

TIP

*The success of this
design depends on rocailles
that are all exactly the
same size.*

3 Pass each end through one rocaille and one 4mm bicone from step 1. Add one 4mm bicone in color B. Cross in one rocaille. Add two 4mm bicones in color A and two rocailles. Pass through the 4mm bicone from step 2. Add one rocaille. Cross in one rocaille as shown. Add two 4mm bicones in color A. Cross in one rocaille. Add one 4mm bicone in color B. Pass through the 4mm bicone and the rocaille from step one. Cross through a 6mm bicone. Begin the band with one 4mm bicone in color B on each thread. Cross in one 4mm bicone in color A. Refer to page 18 to make the band with two rocailles and one faceted oval. Finish symmetrically. Join the threads, and make a knot.

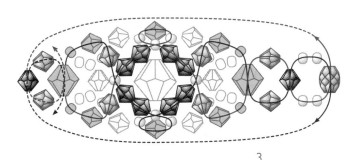

3

Materials

4 bicones, 6mm dia., color A (green)

2 hearts, 10mm x 10mm, color A (green)

8 bicones, 4mm dia., color B (pale green)

1 round bead, 8mm dia., color C (crystal)

14 bicones, 4mm dia., color C (crystal)

2 faceted ovals, 4mm dia., color C (crystal)

2 rondelles, 4mm dia., color C (crystal)

11/0 rocailles, crystal

12 faceted ovals, crystal (for ring band)

56 in. (1.4m) beading thread

2 beading needles

Difficulty ★ ★ ★

TWO-LOVERS RING

1 Center one 4mm bicone in color C on the thread. On each thread end, add one 4mm bicone in color B. Cross in one faceted oval. To each end, add one 4mm bicone in color B, one 4mm bicone in color C, one rocaille, one 6mm bicone, one rocaille, one 4mm bicone in color C, and one 4mm bicone in color B. Cross in one faceted oval. To the top thread (blue), add one 4mm bicone in color B, one 4mm bicone in color C, and one 4mm bicone in color B. Cross through the faceted oval.

2 On each thread, add one rocaille. Pass both ends through the back of one heart, one rocaille, one rondelle, one round bead, one rondelle, one rocaille, and the front of one heart. Add one rocaille to each end. Cross through the faceted oval from step 1. Tighten the threads.

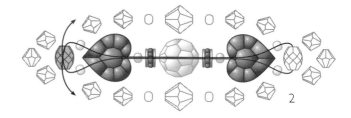

3

Pass each thread through two bicones
from step 1. Add one 4mm bicone in
color C, one 6mm bicone, and one
4mm bicone in color C. Cross in the
round bead. Add one 4mm bicone in
color C. Cross in one 6mm bicone. Add
one 4mm bicone in color C. Follow the
diagram to make the band with two
rocailles and one faceted oval. (See
page 18 for details.) Join the threads,
and make a knot.

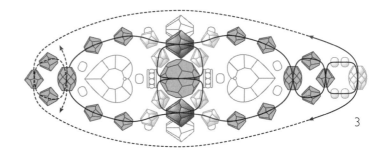

TIP

*It may be necessary to
bend the ring in order to
pass through the round
bead in step 3.*

IRIS RING

  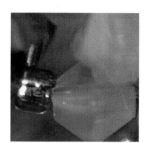

Materials

4 bicone, 6mm dia., color A (turquoise)

14 bicones, 4mm dia., color B (opalescent turquoise)

2 faceted ovals, 6mm dia., color C (blue)

8 bicones, 4mm dia., color C (blue)

2 cubes, 4mm, color C (blue)

3 rondelles, 4mm dia., color C (blue)

11/0 rocailles, turquoise

12 faceted ovals, blue (for ring band)

56 in. (1.4m) beading thread

2 beading needles

Difficulty ★ ★ ★

1 Center one rondelle on the thread. On each end, add one 6mm bicone, one rocaille, one 4mm bicone in color B, one 6mm faceted oval, one 4mm bicone in color B, one rocaille, and one 6mm bicone. Cross in one rondelle.

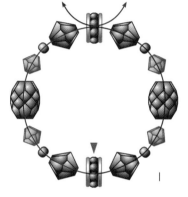

2 Cross each thread through the 6mm bicones from step 1. To each thread, add two 4mm bicones in color A. Pass both threads through one cube, one rondelle, and one cube. Add two 4mm bicones in color A to each thread. Pass the threads as shown in the diagram.

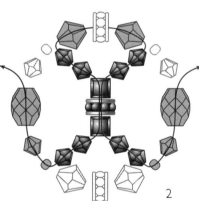

3 On each thread, add two 4mm bicones in color B. Cross through the rondelle. Add two 4mm bicones in color B. Pass through the faceted oval.

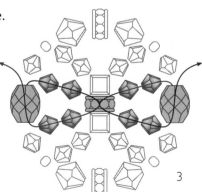

4 Pass the top thread (red) through all of the beads on the outside. Cross through the faceted oval. Refer to page 18 and the diagram (right) to make the band with two rocailles and one faceted oval. Finish symmetrically. Join the threads, and make a knot.

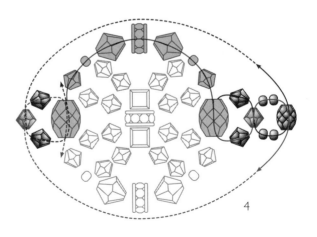

TIP

Be sure to hold the threads evenly while making the ring so that the rondelles remain aligned.

LUCKY-TURTLE PENDANT

Materials

6 faceted ovals, 6mm dia., color A (crystal)

16 bicones, 4mm dia., color B (blue)

13 bicones, 4mm dia., color C (light blue)

11/0 rocailles, blue

Hanging ribbon or cord with findings as desired

48 in. (1.2m) beading thread

2 beading needles

Difficulty: ★ ★ ☆

Technique: The 6-Rose (See page 24.)

1 Make a "6-Rose" by stringing the faceted ovals on the outside and alternating the colors of the center bicones.

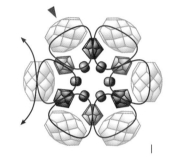

2 On the bottom thread (blue), string one rocaille, one bicone in color C, one bicone in color B, and one bicone in color C. Cross in one rocaille. Pass through the following faceted oval. Repeat for the top thread (red).

3 Repeat step 2, once for the bottom thread (blue) and twice for the top thread (red). Cross through one rocaille. On each end, add one bicone in color C. Cross in one bicone in color B.

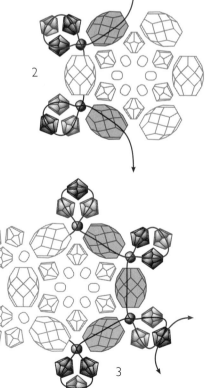

4 | Follow the diagram for adding rocailles and bicones for a hanging loop. Cross in one bicone in color C. Pass each thread through one bicone in color B, continuing as shown. Join the threads; then make a knot.

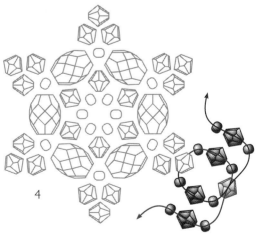

4

TIP
To vary this design you can substitute 6mm bicones for the faceted oval beads.

MOONLIGHT RING

Materials

6 marquise montées, 10mm long, crystal

1 flower, 6mm dia., crystal

12 bicones, 4mm dia., crystal

4 faceted ovals, 3mm dia., crystal

11/0 rocailles, crystal

12 faceted ovals, crystal (for ring band)

52 in. (1.3m) beading thread

2 beading needles

Difficulty: ★ ★ ★

1 | Center five montées on the thread, passing the thread through the inside holes. Cross through the inside holes of another montée. Pass the thread through the outside holes of the same montée.

2 | On each thread end, add one bicone. Pass through the outside hole next to the montée. Repeat twice. Cross though the last montée.

3 | On each thread, string one rocaille and one faceted oval. Pass the threads together through the back of the flower. Add one rocaille. Pass the threads through the flower. On each thread, add one faceted oval and one rocaille. Cross through the montée. To each thread, add a rocaille between the montées, crossing the threads in the top montée.

TIP
You can replace the flower with a 6mm rondelle.

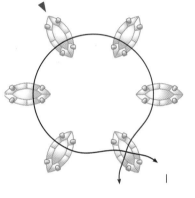

2

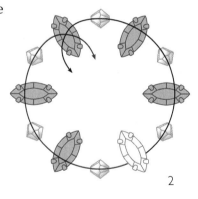

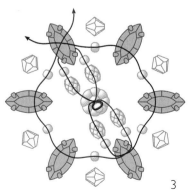

3

4 Pass the top thread (red) through all of the beads on the outside. Cross the threads through the bicone to the left of the montée as shown. On each thread end, add one bicone. Cross through one bicone. Refer to page 18 to make the band with two rocailles and one faceted oval. Finish symmetrically. Join the threads, and make a knot.

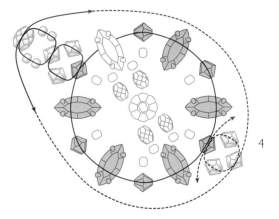

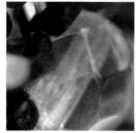

BELLA SET

Ring materials

8 bicones, 4mm dia., color A
(light blue)

8 flowers, 6mm dia., color B (blue)

4 bicones, 6mm dia., color B (blue)

6 bicones, 4mm dia., color B (blue)

4 faceted ovals, 6mm dia., color C
(crystal)

11/0 rocailles, blue

12 faceted ovals, blue
(for ring band)

52 in. (130cm) beading thread

2 beading needles

Difficulty ★ ★ ★

*Technique: The 4-Rose
(See page 22.)*

Ring

1 | Use 4mm bicones to make a "4-Rose." String the first triangle in the center of the thread. Thread two bicones in color B, one rocaille, and one bicone in color A. Cross in the beginning bicone.

2 | Follow the diagram, and string three more triangles. (Color A will be on the outside and color B will be on the inside.)

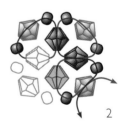

3 | On the right thread (red), add one flower, one rocaille, one 6mm bicone, one rocaille, and one flower. (The flowers will be vertical on the ring.) Pass through two rocailles of the rose. Cross the left thread (blue) through the flower and the rocaille as shown. Pull the threads tight.

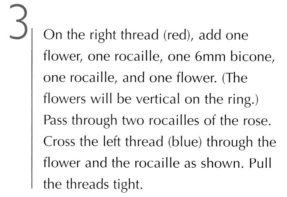

4 | On the right thread (blue), string one faceted oval, one rocaille, and one flower. Pass through one bicone of the rose. Cross the left thread (red) through the flower and one rocaille. Add one 6mm bicone. Repeat the pattern as shown.

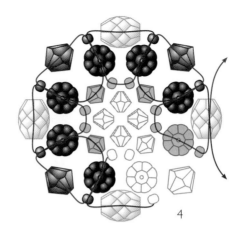

4

5 | Pass the top thread (red) counterclockwise to cross in the bottom faceted oval. Pass the bottom thread (blue) clockwise to cross in the bottom faceted oval. Pull the threads tight to form a ring in a "dome" shape. On each thread end, add one 4mm bicone in color A. Cross in one 4mm bicone in color B. Make the band with two rocailles and one faceted oval. Finish symmetrically. Join the threads, and make a knot.

5

TIP

Have the front of the flowers face toward the center of the ring. In step 3, thread the first flower through the front and the second flower through the back. In step 4, thread all the flowers through the back.

Pendant

Pendant materials

5 bicones, 4mm dia., color A
(light blue)

4 bicones, 6mm dia., color B (blue)

8 flowers, 6mm dia., color B (blue)

4 bicones, 4mm dia., color B (blue)

4 bicones, 6mm dia., color C (crystal)

16 bicones, 4mm dia., color C (crystal)

11/0 rocailles, blue

Hanging ribbon or cord with findings
as desired

28 in. (71.1cm) beading thread

2 beading needles

Difficulty ★ ★ ★

*Technique: The 4-Rose
(See page 22.)*

1 | Follow steps 1–4 of the ring on page 78. Substitute 6mm bicones in color C for the 6mm faceted ovals. Cross in a 6mm bicone in color C.

2 | Pass both threads around the outside. Add one 4mm bicone in color C between each 6mm bicone. Cross in a 6mm bicone at the top. For the loop, add one 4mm bicone in color B, one rocaille, and one 4mm bicone in color B to each thread. Cross in one 4mm bicone in color A. On each thread, add one 4mm bicone in color C, one rocaille, and one 4mm bicone in color C. Cross in the top 6mm bicone. Join the threads, and make a knot.

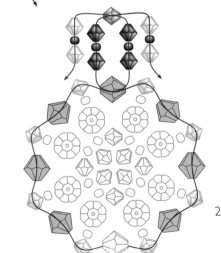

CORALLINE EARRINGS

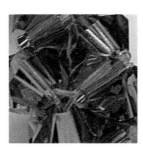
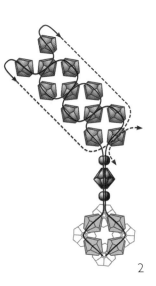

Materials

24 bicones, 4mm dia., color A (opaque turquoise)

2 bicones, 4mm dia., color B (iridescent turquoise)

24 bicones, 4mm dia., color C (turquoise)

11/0 rocailles, turquoise

Hook ear wires, gold

2 strands beading thread, each 16 in. (40.6cm)

2 beading needles

Difficulty ★ ★ ★

1 | Make two earrings. Use bicones in color A for the first ball. Center three bicones on the thread. Cross through one bicone. On each thread, string one bicone. Cross through one bicone. Repeat once. String one bicone on each thread. Cross through the beginning bicone, and pull the threads to make a small ball.

2 | Pass each thread through the two closest bicones. Pass them together through one rocaille and one bicone in color B. Use bicones in color C for the second ball. Pass the left thread (red) through one bicone. Pass the right thread (blue) through two bicones. Cross in one bicone. Pass each thread through one bicone. Cross in the bicone. Repeat once. String one bicone on each thread. Cross through the beginning bicone, and pull the thread to make small ball. Knot the threads. Insert an ear wire through the center of the ball.

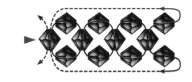

2

TIP
You can elongate this design by adding a third ball.

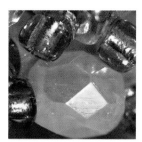

WEDDING RING

Materials

10 faceted ovals, 4mm dia.,
color A (blue)

3 round montées, 4mm dia.,
color A (blue)

8 bicones, 4mm dia.,
color B (crystal)

11/0 rocailles, blue

12 faceted ovals, blue
(for ring band)

48 in. (1.2m) beading thread

2 beading needles

Difficulty ★ ★ ★

*Technique: The Square Cross
(See page 20.)*

1 Make a row of three squares as shown. Cross in the last faceted oval. String one rocaille on each thread. Cross in one montée. String one rocaille on each thread. Cross in a faceted oval. Repeat twice.

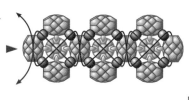

1

2 String one rocaille on each thread. Pass through the faceted ovals. On the bottom thread (red), string two rocailles, one bicone, and two rocailles. Pass through the faceted oval in the middle. Add one rocaille, and pass through the faceted oval. Add one rocaille, and pass through the faceted oval. Add one rocaille. Cross through the last faceted oval. On the top thread (blue), add one rocaille. Pass through the faceted oval. Add two rocailles, one bicone, and and two rocailles. Pass through the faceted oval in the middle. Add one rocaille, and pass through the faceted oval. Add one rocaille. Cross in the last faceted oval.

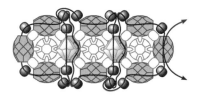

2

TIP
For a firm, stable ring, after the band is finished, pass all the threads back through the rocaille and montées before knotting them.

3 | String one bicone on each thread. Cross
in one bicone. Refer to page 18 to make
a band with two rocailles and one
faceted oval. Finish symmetrically. Join
the threads, and make a knot.

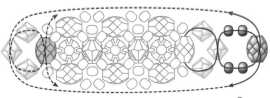

3

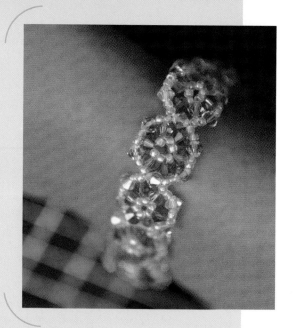

ROBYN BRACELET

Materials

51 bicones, 4mm dia., color A (light yellow)

30 bicones, 4mm dia., color B (yellow)

3 bicones, 6mm dia., color B (yellow)

30 bicones, 4mm dia., color C (deep yellow)

11/0 rocailles, light yellow

80 in. (2.0m) beading thread

2 beading needles

(These beads will make 10 roses.)

Difficulty ★ ★ ★

Techniques: Assembling Picks (See page 17.) The 6-Rose (See page 24.)

1. Make a "Six-Rose" alternating 4mm bicones in colors B and C at the center. String the 4mm bicones in color A on the outside.

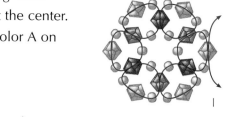

2. On the bottom thread (blue), string one rocaille, one 4mm bicone in color B, one rocaille, and one 4mm bicone in color C. On the top thread (red), add one rocaille, and cross through the last bicone strung. Make the triangles as shown, and cross in a bicone in color A.

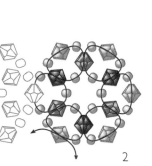

3. Pass and cross the threads as shown. Cross in the bicone in color A at the right.

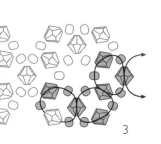

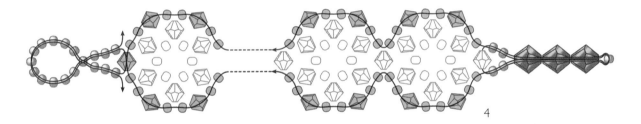

4

4 Repeat steps 2–3 to make 10 roses (or enough roses to make the desired length). String two rocailles on each thread. To make the pick, pass both threads through three 6mm bicones and one rocaille. Pass the threads back through the 6mm bicones and two rocailles. Pass each thread through the outside bicones and rocailles to the other end of bracelet. Cross in the 4mm bicone. On each thread, string three rocailles. Cross in one rocaille. String 11 rocailles on one thread. Cross the other thread through the 11 rocailles. Cross the threads in one rocaille. Pass each thread through the following rocailles. Pass the threads through several beads to join them. Make a knot, and trim the ends.

TIP

This bracelet doesn't need a clasp or other finding. To fasten, slip the bicone pick into the loop.

PETALS SET

Pendant materials

6 hearts, 10mm x 10mm, color A (yellow)

6 faceted ovals, 4mm dia., color A (yellow)

7 bicones, 4mm dia., color A (yellow)

6 bicones, 4mm dia., color B (white opal)

11/0 rocailles, pale yellow

Hanging ribbon or cord with findings as desired

48 in. (1.2m) beading thread

2 beading needles

Difficulty ★ ★ ★

Technique: The 6-Rose (See page 24.)

Pendant

String one heart on the center of the thread. (Be sure to string all hearts so they are face up.) On each thread, add one rocaille. On the bottom thread, string one faceted oval and one rocaille. On the top thread, string one bicone in color B and one rocaille. Cross through one heart and the opposite rocailles. Repeat this four times. String the bicone in color B on the top thread and the faceted oval on the bottom thread. Cross the threads through the first rocailles and the first heart. (Have the threads exit on the opposite sides of the heart.)

TIP
The challenge of this design is creating the flower shape. The hearts must be strung correctly, and the threads kept tight so that the shape remains stable.

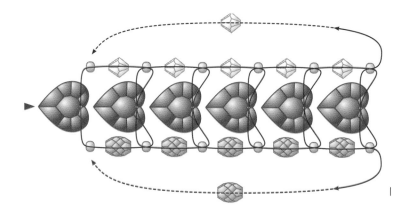

2 | Tighten the threads, and at the same time, turn the tips of the hearts to the outside. Pass the bottom thread (blue) counterclockwise through five faceted ovals and the following rocaille.

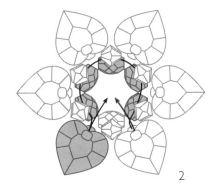

2

3 | On the right thread (red), string one bicone in color A, one rocaille, and one bicone in color A. Pass through the bicone in color B from the previous step. Pass the left thread (blue) through the second bicone in color A.

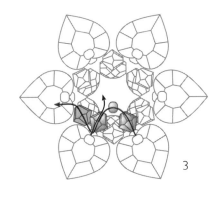

3

4 | On the right thread (blue), place one rocaille and one bicone in color A. Pass through the bicone in color B from the previous step. Cross the left thread (red) through the second bicone in color A. To this thread, add one rocaille and one bicone in color A. Pass through the bicone in color B. Repeat, crossing through the bicone in color B from the previous step.

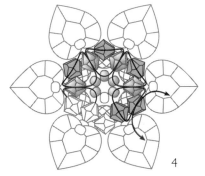

4

5 | Pass each thread through one rocaille and one heart to the back of the assembly. Pass each thread through the faceted ovals. Cross in the last faceted oval as shown. For the loop, string five rocailles on each thread. Cross through one bicone in color A. Add five rocailles to each thread. Cross through the faceted oval on the front. Pass through several beads on the back to join the threads, and make a knot.

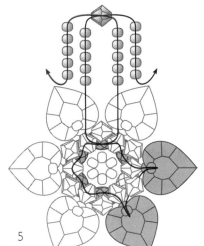

5

PETALS SET

Ring

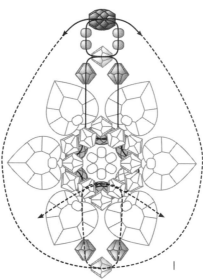

Follow steps 1–4 of the pendant on page 88. Pass each thread through the ovals at the back. Cross in the last oval. On each thread, add one bicone in color A. Cross in one bicone in color B. Refer to page 18 and the diagram to make the band with two rocailles and one faceted oval. Finish symmetrically. Join the threads; then make a knot.

Earrings

Make two earrings. On the ear wire, add two rocailles, one bicone in color B, one rocaille, and one bicone in color A. String one heart on the thread's center. Pass both threads in one rocaille and one bicone in color B. On each, add one rocaille and one bicone in color A. Pass both threads in one rocaille. On each thread, add one bicone in color A, three rocailles, one bicone in color B, and four rocailles. Pass the left thread (red) through the beads on the ear wire, three rocailles, the bicone in color B, and four rocailles. Add one rocaille to the thread. Cross the right thread (blue) in four rocailles, the bicone in color B, and three rocailles. Cross the right thread in the beads on the ear wire. Pass both threads through the next bicone, and knot them.

TIP

For longer earrings, add more bicones above the heart.

Ring materials

6 hearts, 10mm x 10mm, color A (yellow)

6 faceted ovals, 4mm dia., color A (yellow)

10 bicones, 4mm dia., color A (yellow)

8 bicones, 4mm dia., color B (white opal)

11/0 rocailles, light yellow

12 faceted ovals, yellow (for ring band)

48 in. (1.2m) beading thread

2 beading needles

Difficulty ★ ★ ★

Earring materials

2 hearts, 10mm x 10mm, color A (yellow)

10 bicones, 4mm dia., color A (yellow)

8 bicones, 4mm dia., color B (white opal)

11/0 rocailles, pale yellow

Hook ear wires, silver

2 strands beading thread, each 12 in. (30.5cm)

2 beading needles

Difficulty ★ ★ ★

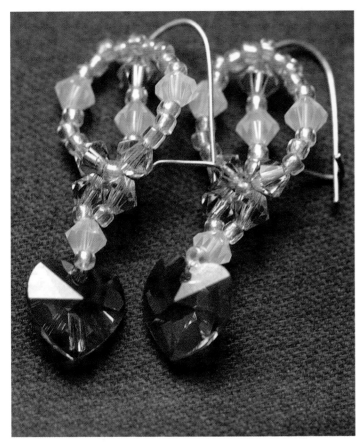

GEOMETRIC RING

Materials

1 round bead, 8mm dia., color A (crystal)

2 cubes, 6mm, color A (crystal)

4 cubes, 4mm, color A (crystal)

12 bicones, 4mm dia., color B (light blue)

11/0 rocailles, light blue

12 faceted ovals, light blue (for ring band)

24 in. (61.0cm) beading thread

2 beading needles

Difficulty ★ ★ ★

1 | On the center of the thread, string one 6mm cube. On each thread, string one 4mm cube. Cross though the 8mm round bead. On each thread end, add one 4mm cube. Cross through one 6mm cube.

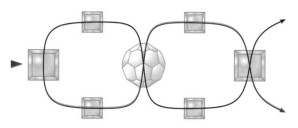

2 | On each thread, add four rocailles. Cross through one rocaille. String four rocailles on each thread. Cross through the round bead. On each thread, add four rocailles. Cross in one rocaille. Add four rocailles on each thread. Cross in one 6mm cube.

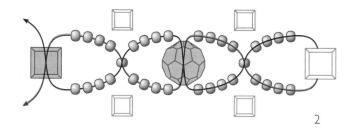

3 | Pass through all the cubes, placing one bicone between each. Refer to page 18 and the diagram to make the band with the bicones and rocailles. Finish symmetrically. Join the threads, and knot them.

TIP
Always use beautiful, perfectly made rocailles.

3

EMERALD EARRINGS

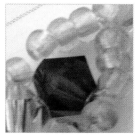  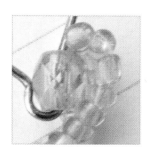

Materials

10 bicones, 4mm dia., color A (dark green)

10 bicones, 4mm dia., color B (light green)

4 faceted ovals, 4mm dia., color B (light green)

11/0 rocailles, light green

Hook ear wires, gold

2 strands beading thread, each 12 in. (30.5cm)

2 beading needles

Difficulty ★ ★ ★

Technique: The 5-Rose (See page 23.)

Make two earrings. Make a "5-Rose," stringing the bicones in color A on the outside and the bicones in color B on the inside. Cross through the bicone in color A. To each thread, add three rocailles. Pass both threads through one faceted oval. Thread one faceted oval on the ear wire. Pass both threads through the faceted oval on the ear wire. On each thread, add five rocailles. Pass through the second faceted oval from the top. Pass through the rocailles and the bicones, and join the ends together on the back. Knot the threads.

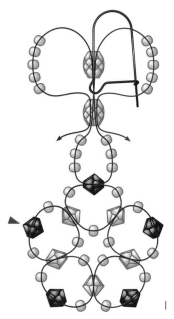

TIP
After knotting the threads, pass the ends through the beads again to conceal them.

LIGHTNING RING

Materials

18 faceted ovals, 2mm dia.,
color A (sky blue)

12 bicones, 4mm dia.,
color A (sky blue)

12 bicones, 4mm dia.,
color B (turquoise)

11/0 rocailles, white

12 faceted ovals, sky blue
(for ring band)

28 in. (71.1cm) beading thread

2 beading needles

Difficulty ★ ★ ★

*Technique: The Square Cross
(See page 20.)*

1 | Use faceted ovals to make two columns of three squares, staggering them.

2 | On the right column, thread three bicone flowers as shown, alternating bicones in colors A and B. Place one rocaille in the middle.

3 | Pass the threads as shown in diagram 3a. Thread three bicone flowers on the left column as shown in diagram 3b.

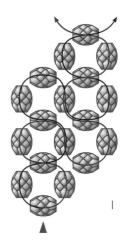

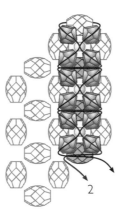

2

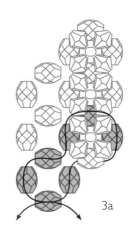

3a

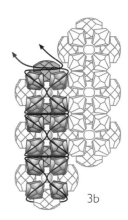

3b

4 Pass each thread through the outside faceted ovals, inserting one rocaille between the beads as shown. Cross in the last rocaille at the bottom right.

5 Pass each thread through a faceted oval. To each thread, add three rocailles. Cross in the last rocaille from step 4. Pass through the third rocaille on the strand. Cross back through the last rocaille from step 4. To each thread, add one rocaille. Cross in the first faceted oval of the band. Refer to page 18 to make a band with two rocailles and one faceted oval. Finish symmetrically. Join the threads; then make a knot.

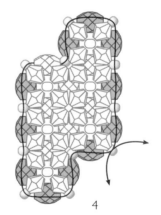

4

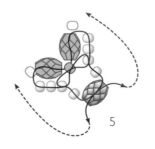

5

TIP

For a ring that is centered vertically, begin the band on the middle faceted oval on the right. Finish by attaching the band to the first faceted oval on the left.

Autumn

When the days of summer are at an end and autumn makes itself known in glowing colors and soft silhouettes, capture a little extra sparkle with vivid jewelry inspired by the season. Drape your wrist with the "Sunset" bracelet; encircle your finger with the "Flower Basket" ring; or adorn yourself with the "Exquisite" earrings and ring. In a moment, autumn's unique palette will add understated style and sophistication to your wardrobe.

ROSE-WINDOW RING

Materials

4 faceted ovals, 4mm dia., color A
(khaki)

8 bicones, 4mm dia., color A
(khaki)

12 faceted ovals, 4mm dia.,
color C (light brown)

8 bicones, 4mm dia., color B
(ochre)

11/0 rocailles, gold

12 faceted ovals, ochre
(for ring band)

52 in. (1.3m) beading thread

2 beading needles

Difficulty

*Technique: The 6-Rose
(See page 24.)*

1　Make one "6-Rose" using 12 faceted
ovals in color C. Cross in one faceted
oval.

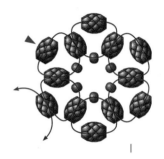

2　Pass both threads through the outside
faceted ovals, inserting one bicone
in color A after each. Cross in one
faceted oval.

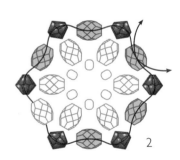

3　On each thread, string one faceted oval
in color A and one bicone in color B.
Cross through one rocaille. On each
thread, string one bicone in color B
and one faceted oval in color A. Cross
through the faceted oval. Begin the
band as shown. Continue with rocailles
and faceted ovals. End symmetrically.
Join the threads; then knot.

TIP
*For a chunkier design,
replace the center
faceted ovals with
6mm bicones.*

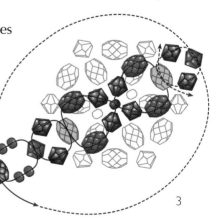

EXQUISITE SET

Earring Materials

4 bicones, 6mm dia., color A (light brown)

4 bicones, 4mm dia., color A (light brown)

4 faceted ovals, 6mm dia., color B (brown)

20 bicones, 4mm dia., color C (gold)

11/0 rocailles, gold

Hook ear wires, gold

2 strands beading thread, each 16 in. (40.6cm)

2 beading needles

Difficulty ★ ★ ★

Earrings

1 On the thread, center one 6mm bicone. Following the diagram, add the 4mm bicones in color C and the faceted ovals.

2 Pass and cross the threads through the 4mm bicones. On each thread, add one rocaille. Pass the threads together through one 4mm bicone in color A, one rocaille, and one 4mm bicone in color A. On each thread, string one rocaille. Pass and cross the threads through the bicones as shown.

3 On each thread, string three rocailles. Cross the thread through the hole in the ear wire. On each thread, string one rocaille and one 4mm bicone in color C. Cross through one rocaille. On each thread, add one 4mm bicone in color C and one rocaille. Cross through one rocaille. Cross the threads around the ear wire. Pass the threads through the beads, and knot them.

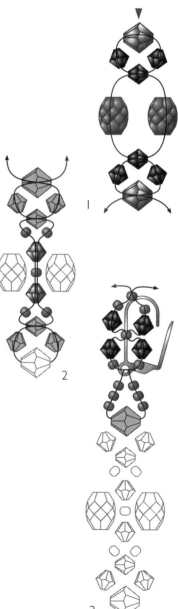

Ring

1 On the thread, center three 4mm bicones and one 6mm bicone color A as shown. Pass the ends through the 4mm bicone. On each thread, add one faceted oval, one 4mm bicone, and one faceted oval. Cross the ends in one 4mm bicone. On each thread, add one 4mm bicone. Cross in one 6mm bicone in color A.

2 Pass each thread in the 4mm bicones. Cross in a 4mm bicone. On each thread, add one rocaille. To both threads, add one rocaille, one 6mm bicone in color D, one rocaille, one 6mm bicone in color D, and one rocaille. On each thread, add one rocaille. Pass the top thread (blue) in the 4mm and the 6mm bicones. Cross in a 4mm bicone. Cross the bottom thread (red) in a 4mm bicone.

3 Pass each thread as shown. On the top thread (red), add two rocailles and one 6mm bicone in color D. Cross the ends in one rocaille. Add one 6mm bicone in color D and two rocailles. Cross in a 4mm bicone. On the bottom thread (blue), string one rocaille. Cross through one rocaille, one 6mm bicone, one rocaille, one 6mm bicone, and one rocaille. Add one rocaille. Cross in a 4mm bicone.

4 Pass the bottom thread (red) at the right as shown. On each thread, string one 4mm

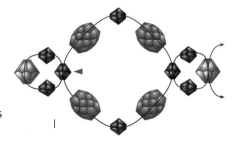

1

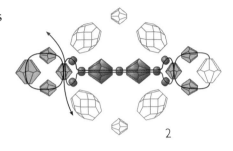

2

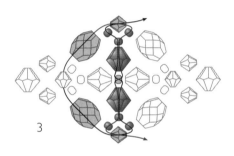

3

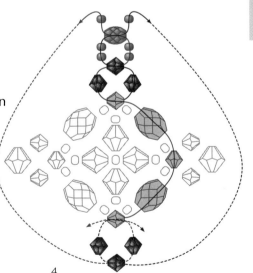

4

TIP

In steps 2 and 3, be sure that the threads that pass through the 6mm bicones are held tight.

bicone. Cross in one 4mm bicone. Begin the band as shown. Continue with rocailles and faceted ovals. End symmetrically. Join the threads; then knot them.

EXQUISITE SET

Pendant

1 Follow step 1 of the ring on page 103, adding the 4mm and 6mm bicones at the top and bottom as shown. Cross through a 4mm bicone.

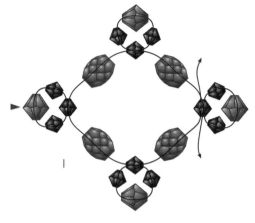

2 On each thread, add one rocaille. To both threads, add one rocaille, one 6mm bicone in color D, one rocaille, one 6mm bicone in color D, and one rocaille. On each thread, add one rocaille. Pass the top thread (blue) through a 4mm bicone, a faceted oval, and a 4mm bicone. Cross the bottom thread (red) through a 4mm bicone. Pass it through a faceted oval and a 4mm bicone.

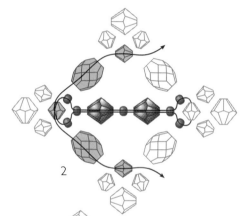

3 String the center vertical beads as shown in the diagram.

4 Pass each thread through a faceted oval. Cross in a 4mm bicone. Pass each thread through a 4 mm bicone. Cross in a 6mm bicone. For the loop, string five rocailles on each thread. Cross in a 4mm bicone. Add five rocailles to each thread. Cross in a 6mm bicone. Pass through the beads to join the threads, and knot them.

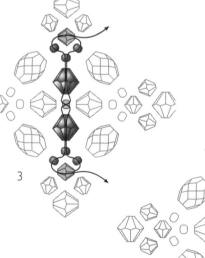

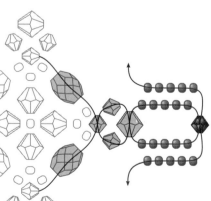

Pendant Materials

4 bicones, 6mm dia., color A (dark brown)

4 bicones, 6mm dia., color B (light brown)

4 faceted ovals, 6mm dia., color C (brown)

13 bicones, 4mm dia., color D (gold)

11/0 rocailles, gold

Hanging ribbon or cord with findings as desired

40 in. (1.0m) beading thread

2 beading needles

Difficulty ★ ★ ★

GOTHIC-CROSS PENDANT

Materials

9 bicones, 4mm dia., color A (dark burgundy)

8 bicones, 6mm dia., color B (burgundy)

24 faceted ovals, 4mm dia., color B (burgundy)

1 cube, 6mm, color B (burgundy)

6 bicones, 4mm dia., color C (khaki)

4 cubes, 4mm, color C (khaki)

4 bicones, 6mm dia., color C (khaki)

11/0 rocailles, khaki

Hanging ribbon or cord with findings as desired

56 in. (1.4m) beading thread

2 beading needles

Difficulty ★ ★ ★

Technique: The Square Cross (See page 20.)

1. On the center of the thread, make the first triangle using one 6mm bicone in color B, two rocailles, and two 4mm bicones in color A. Cross through one rocaille. Working to the right, use faceted ovals to make a diagonal row of three squares. Before completing the third square, use the right thread (blue) to make a second triangle; then finish the the square. Make a diagonal row of squares, working from the bottom right to the top left. On the top thread (red), string one faceted oval, and make the third triangle. Make the last diagonal row of squares. Cross in one rocaille.

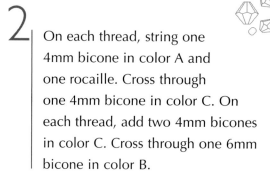

2. On each thread, string one 4mm bicone in color A and one rocaille. Cross through one 4mm bicone in color C. On each thread, add two 4mm bicones in color C. Cross through one 6mm bicone in color B.

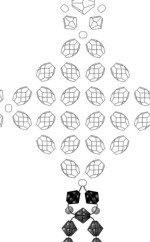

3 On each end, add two rocailles. Pass both ends in one 4mm cube. On each end, add two rocailles. Cross in the bicone underneath. On each end, add one rocaille. Pass both in one 4mm bicone in color C and one rocaille. Cross in one rocaille underneath. Pass the right thread (blue) in the right ovals, adding one rocaille between each. Pass in a rocaille at the right. Add eight rocailles and one 4mm cube as shown. Pass in an oval. Pass the left thread (red) in the bottom left oval. String the rocailles and the 6mm bicones as shown.

4 On the bottom thread (red), string one rocaille, one 6mm bicone in color C, and one rocaille. Pass in an oval. Add two rocailles, a 6mm cube, and two rocailles. Pass in an oval. Add two rocailles. Pass in a cube. Add two rocailles. Pass in two ovals. Add one rocaille, one 6mm bicone in color C, and one rocaille. Pass in an oval. Add one rocaille. Pass in an oval. Repeat. On the top thread (blue), add one rocaille. Pass in an oval. Repeat. Pass in the top rocaille. Add one rocaille, one 4mm cube, and one rocaille. Pass in the top bicone. Add one rocaille. Pass in the cube. Add one rocaille. Cross in the next rocaille. Add one rocaille. Pass in an oval. Repeat. Pass in the left rocaille.

5 On the top thread (blue), add two rocailles, one 4mm cube, and two rocailles. Pass in a bicone at the tip. Add two rocailles. Pass in the cube. Add two rocailles. Pass in the beads as shown. On the bottom thread (red), string the rocailles and 6mm bicones as shown. Pass in the beads as shown. On each thread, string four rocailles for the loop. Cross in one 4mm bicone in color B. String four rocailles on each end. Cross in the top bicone. Pass in the beads to join the threads, and knot them.

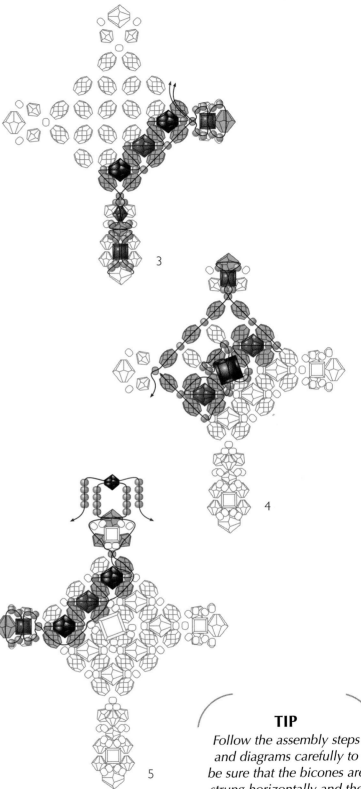

TIP

Follow the assembly steps and diagrams carefully to be sure that the bicones are strung horizontally and the cubes are strung vertically.

Materials

24 bicones, 4mm dia., color A (ochre)

3 flowers, 6mm dia., color A (ochre)

3 hearts, 10mm x 10mm, color A (ochre)

20 bicones, 4mm dia., color B (light brown)

20 bicones, 4mm dia., color C (dark brown)

11/0 rocailles, brass

2 bead tips, 2 jump rings, and 1 gold lobster-claw clasp

48 in. (1.2m) beading thread

2 beading needles

Difficulty ★ ★ ★

Techniques: Bead Tips (See page 12.) Clasps and Jump Rings (See page 13.)

SUNSET BRACELET

Note: The "Sunset" bracelet is composed of a pattern of five bicone flowers on each end section and a pattern of one heart/flower pendant, three bicone flowers, one heart/flower pendant, three bicone flowers, and one heart/flower pendant for the center section.

1 Center one rocaille on the thread. Make a knot below the rocaille. On each thread, string one rocaille and one bicone in color A. Cross in one rocaille. On each thread, string one bicone in color A, one rocaille, and one bicone in color B. Cross in one rocaille. On each thread, string one bicone in color B, one rocaille, and one bicone in color C. Cross in one rocaille. Repeat the pattern, and make five bicone flowers in alternating colors as shown. Secure the bead tip over the first rocaille.

2 On the left thread (red), string four rocailles, one heart, and one rocaille. Pass back through the heart and one rocaille. Add three rocailles, one bicone in color C, and one rocaille. On the right thread (blue), string one rocaille, one flower, and one rocaille. Pass through the flower. Add one rocaille and one bicone in color C. Cross in one rocaille. (Be sure that the heart is face up and that the right side of the flower faces away from the bracelet.)

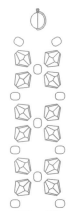

3

(a) On each thread, string on one bicone in color C, one rocaille, and one bicone in color A. Cross the ends through one rocaille. On each thread, string on one bicone in color A, one rocaille, and one bicone in color B. Cross the ends through one rocaille. On each thread, string on one bicone in color B. Repeat step 2 to add a heart/flower pendant. (b) Repeat step 3a and step 2 to make three bicone flowers and one heart/flower pendant. (c) On each thread, string on one bicone in color C. Following the color sequence (ochre-light brown-dark brown), string four more bicone flowers, ending with a bicone flower in color A. To each thread, add one rocaille. Cross in one rocaille. Knot and trim the thread ends. Secure the bead tip over the rocaille. Attach the jump rings to each bead tip. Attach the clasp to one jump ring.

TIP

If you have a small wrist, make four bicone flowers at each end of the bracelet instead of five as shown.

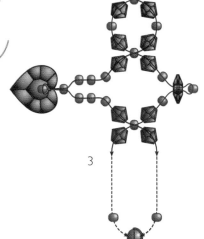

3

LOVE PENDANT

Materials

1 heart, 30mm x 30mm or 50mm x 50mm, crystal

20 bicones, 4mm dia., color A (gold)

16 bicones, 4mm dia., color B (light brown)

Hanging ribbon or cord with findings as desired

40 in. (1.0m) beading thread

2 beading needles

Difficulty

Technique: The Square Cross (See page 20.)

1 | Beginning on the center of the thread, make one column of five squares from bicones. (Follow the diagram for placement of the bicone colors. Cross the threads as shown.)

2 | Pass the right thread (red) as shown, and make the second column. Pass the left thread (blue), and make the third column. Pass and cross the threads through the bicones.

3 | Begin the fourth column with the bottom thread (red), and continue using both threads. Cross through the bicones as shown.

4 | Pass the top and bottom threads to make a fifth column. Cross in the last bicone.

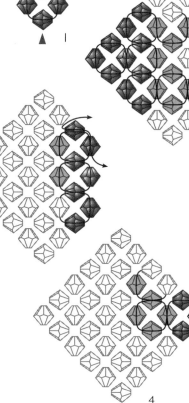

5

Pass both threads through the hole in the heart so that they exit on the right side of the heart. Cross the threads through the bicone at the opposite tip of the square. Tighten the threads. (The square will curve over the top of the heart.) Pass the threads again through the hole in the heart to the wrong side of the heart. Cross them again in the bottom bicone. Pass the threads through several beads until they join. Knot the threads, and conceal the knot in a bicone.

5

GYPSY RING

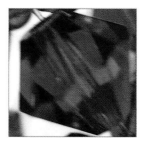

Materials

1 bicone, 6mm dia,. color A
(fuchsia)

4 bicones, 4mm dia., color A
(fuchsia)

1 bicone, 6mm dia., color B
(khaki)

4 bicones, 4mm dia., color B
(khaki)

4 bicones, 4mm dia., color C
(orange)

4 bicones, 4mm dia., color D
(ochre)

11/0 rocailles in yellow

12 faceted ovals, yellow
(for ring band)

48 in. (1.2m) beading thread

2 beading needles

Difficulty ★ ★ ★

1 | On the thread (red), center one rocaille, one 4mm bicone in color D, one rocaille, one 4mm bicone in color B, one rocaille, and one 4mm bicone in color A. Cross through the first rocaille. Add one 6mm bicone in color B and one rocaille. On the bottom thread (blue), string one 4mm bicone in color B, one rocaille, one 4mm bicone in color A, one rocaille, and one bicone in color C. Cross through one rocaille. (There will be two circles of beads.)

2 | On the top thread (blue), string one 4mm bicone in color D, one rocaille, one 4mm bicone in color B, one rocaille, and one 4mm bicone in color C. On the bottom thread (red), string one 6mm bicone in color A, one rocaille, one 4mm bicone in color C, one rocaille, one 4mm bicone in color A, one rocaille, and one 4mm bicone in color D. Pass through the rocaille as shown. Pass the top thread (blue) as shown.

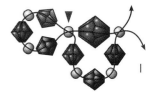

3 | Pass the left thread (red) through the beads as shown. Cross in the first 4mm bicone in color B on the left. On the right thread (blue), string one 4mm bicone in color B, one rocaille, one 4mm bicone in color D, and one rocaille. Pass through one bicone, one rocaille, and one bicone in the middle. Add one rocaille, one 4mm bicone in color A, one rocaille, and one 4mm bicone in color C. Cross through one rocaille. Pass through the beads. Cross in the first 4mm bicone in color B on the right. Make a band using two rocailles on each thread. Cross in one faceted oval. Join the threads, and knot them. (See page 18.)

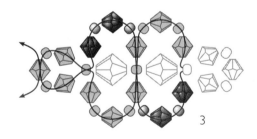

3

TIP

The colors of this design can be easily changed, but to retain the contrast, choose at least three different colors.

WILDFLOWER RING

Materials

4 double bicones, 15mm long, color A (ochre)

3 round beads, 8mm dia., color B (brown)

3 round beads, 6mm dia., color C (dark brown)

11/0 rocailles, dark brown

12 faceted ovals, brown (for ring band)

4 20-in. (50.8cm) strands and 9 8-in. (20.3cm) strands beading thread

2 beading needles

Difficulty ★ ★ ★

Technique: Assembling Picks (See page 17.)

I | Begin the ring band by knotting the four 20-in. strands together 6 in. (15.2cm) from one end. On each longer doubled thread, string two rocailles. Cross in one faceted oval. For the band pattern, on each thread string one rocaille. Cross in one faceted oval. Repeat the pattern to the desired length, ending with two rocailles. Pull the threads tight, and knot the ends together to complete the band. (Do not cut the ends.)

2 | Assemble the beads using the pick technique on page 17. On two 8-in.-long threads, string one double bicone and one rocaille. Pass through one double bicone. Tighten, then knot the thread with the other threads on the underside of the assembly.

TIP

Apply glue or clear nail polish to the knots, and let them dry. This will keep the beads and knots stable during assembly.

2

3 | Repeat to make three more picks. Pass the threads through the beads in the band. Cut the ends.

4 | Working from the underside, insert the ends of one 8-in. (20.3cm) strand on either side of one rocaille. With the ends even, string one 6mm round bead and one rocaille. Pass through the round bead. Repeat with two 6mm round beads and three 8mm round beads. Knot the threads on the underside. Conceal the ends.

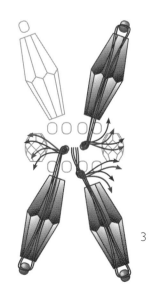

3

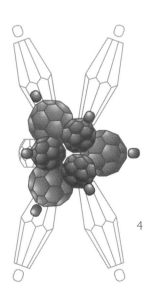

4

INDIAN-SUMMER PENDANT

Materials

5 bicones, 6mm dia, color A (brown)

8 bicones, 4mm dia., color A (brown)

8 bicones, 6mm dia., color B (khaki)

1 round montée, 6mm dia., color B (khaki)

4 bicones, 6mm dia., color C (ochre)

7 bicones, 4mm dia., color C (ochre)

1 rhinestone rondell, 6mm dia., color D (crystal)

11/0 rocailles, gold

Hanging ribbon or cord with findings as desired

48 in. (1.2m) beading thread

2 beading needles

Difficulty ★ ★ ★

Technique: The 8-Rose (See page 24.)

1 Make an "8-Rose." String the first triangle in the center of the thread. Thread one 6mm bicone in color B, one rocaille, one 6mm bicone in color A, and one 4mm bicone in color A. Cross in one 6mm bicone in color C. Make seven more triangles. Cross in a 6mm bicone in color B.

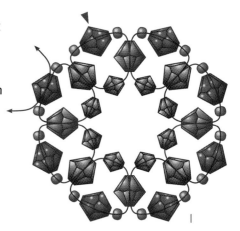

2 Pass the top thread (blue) through the outside beads, adding one rocaille between every two rocailles. At the second and fourth rocaille additions, thread one 4mm bicone in color C, one rocaille, and one 4mm bicone in color C. Cross through the rocaille. Repeat with the bottom thread (red). Cross the threads as shown, and pass through the beads to the center of the bicones. Pass the top thread (red) around the center bicones, adding one rocaille between each. Cross the threads as shown.

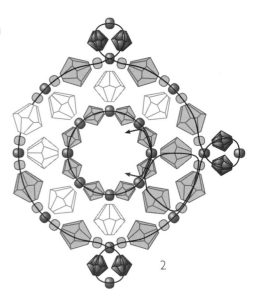

TIP
To change the look of this pendant, substitute khaki or ochre rocailles.

3 On each thread, string one rocaille. Cross through the montée. String one rocaille on each thread. Cross and pass through the beads as shown.

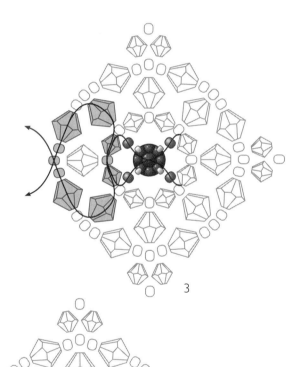

3

4 For the loop, pass both threads through one rhinestone rondell and one 6mm bicone in color A. On each thread, add five rocailles. Cross in one 4mm bicone in color C. On each thread, add five rocailles. Pass through a 6mm bicone and the rondell. Join the threads, and knot them.

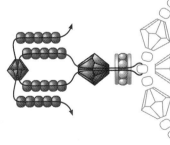

4

WALLFLOWER RING

Materials

8 bicones, 4mm dia., color A (ochre)

1 marquise montée, 15mm long, color A (ochre)

2 bicones, 6mm dia., color B (khaki)

2 bicones, 4mm dia., color B (khaki)

10 bicones, 4mm dia., color C (dark purple)

11/0 rocailles, yellow

12 faceted ovals, yellow (for ring band)

52 in. (1.3m) beading thread

2 beading needles

Difficulty   ★ ★ ★

1 | On the center of the thread, string one 6mm bicone. On each thread end, string one rocaille, one 4mm bicone in color A, one rocaille, one 4mm bicone in color B, and one 4mm bicone in color C. Pass through the montée. Add one 4mm bicone in color C. Pass through the 4mm bicone in color B.

2 | On each thread, string one rocaille, one 4mm bicone in color A, and one rocaille. Cross through one 6mm bicone.

3 | To each thread, add one rocaille and one 4mm bicone in color C. Cross through the montée. On each thread, add one 4mm bicone in color C and one rocaille. Cross through the 6mm bicone.

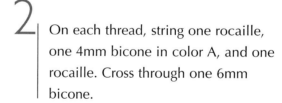
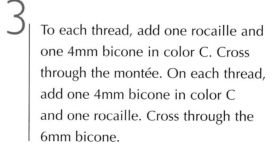
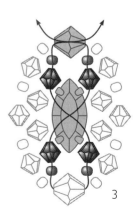

4 Pass the threads through the outside beads to the 4mm bicone at the right. On each thread, add one 4mm bicone in color A. Cross in one 4mm bicone in color D. Continue the band with rocailles and faceted ovals. End symmetrically. Join the threads, and knot them.

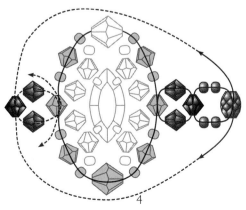

4

TIP

For a two-color version of this ring, replace the bicones in color C with bicones in color A.

FLOWER-BASKET RING

Materials

6 bicones, 6mm dia., color A (light burgundy)

12 bicones, 4mm dia., color B (khaki)

1 round montée, 6mm dia., color B (khaki)

10 bicones, 4mm dia., color C (ochre)

10 bicones, 4mm dia., color D (dark burgundy)

11/0 rocailles, yellow

12 faceted ovals, light burgundy (for ring band)

48 in. (1.2m) beading thread

2 beading needles

Difficulty ★ ★ ★

1 | On the thread, center one 4mm bicone in color C. On each thread, string one 4mm bicone in color D, one rocaille, and one 6mm bicone. Cross through the montée. On each thread, string one 6mm bicone and one rocaille. Cross in one 4mm bicone in color C.

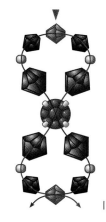

2 | Pass each thread through one bicone and one rocaille. On each thread, string one 4mm bicone in color B, one rocaille, one 6mm bicone, one rocaille, and one 4mm bicone in color B. Pass through one rocaille and one 4mm bicone. Cross through one 4mm bicone.

3 | On each thread, string one 4mm bicone in color B. Cross in one rocaille. Add one 4mm bicone in color D. Cross in the montée. Repeat the pattern, reversing the colors. Cross in the bottom 4mm bicone. Pass through the beads on the outside; then pass through to the center 6mm bicone.

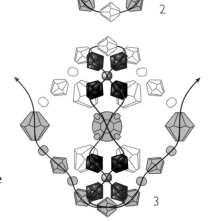

4

On the right thread (blue), string one bicone in color B, one rocaille, and one bicone in color C. Cross in a montée. String the same beads, reversing the colors. Cross in the left 6mm bicone. Repeat with the left thread (blue). Cross in the right 6mm bicone.

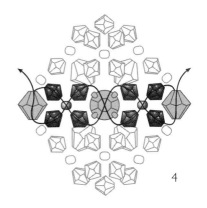

4

5

Pass and cross each thread in the 4mm bicone at the top. On each thread, string one 4mm bicone in color C. Cross in one 4mm bicone in color D. Continue the band with the rocailles and faceted ovals. End symmetrically. Join the threads, and knot them.

TIP
Hold the threads tight throughout the assembly, especially in steps 3 and 4.

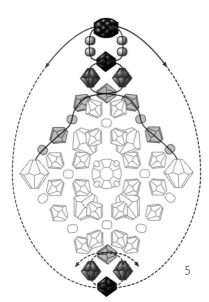

5

DIANE EARRINGS

Materials

22 bicones, 4mm dia., color A (khaki)

12 bicones, 4mm dia, color B (light brown)

18 faceted ovals, 4mm dia., color C (brown)

11/0 rocailles, khaki

Hook ear wires, silver

2 crimp tubes, 2mm x 2mm, silver

Crimping pliers

2 strands beading thread, each 24 in. (61.0cm)

2 beading needles

Difficulty ★ ★ ★

Techniques: Assembling Picks (See page 17.)
The Square Cross (See page 20.)

1 On the center of the thread, make the first square using four faceted ovals. Cross in the top right oval. Begin the flower on the top thread (blue) by stringing one bicone in color B, one rocaille, and one bicone in color B. Cross in the bottom left oval. On the bottom thread (red), string one bicone in color A. Cross in the rocaille. String one bicone in color A. Cross in the bottom left oval.

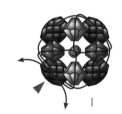

2 On the top thread (blue), string one rocaille. Pass through the faceted oval. Repeat. On the bottom thread (red), string two bicones in color A and one rocaille. Pass through the bicones to make a pick. Pass through the faceted oval. On both threads, string two rocailles. Make a second square of faceted ovals.

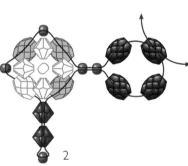

3 On the thread (red), string one bicone in color B, one rocaille, one bicone in color B. Pass through two ovals at the left. On the thread (blue), add one bicone

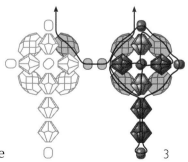

in color A. Pass in the rocaille and add one bicone in color A. Pass through the oval. Add two bicones in color A and one rocaille. Pass through the pick and one oval. Add one rocaille. Pass through the oval. Add one rocaille. Pass through one oval, two rocailles, and one oval.

4 On each thread, string one bicone in color A and one rocaille. Cross through one bicone in color B. On each thread, string two rocailles. Pass both threads through one rocaille. On the ear wire, thread one rocaille and one faceted oval. Pass both threads through both beads on the ear wire. On each thread, string five rocailles. Pass both threads through the first rocaille below the ear wire, and knot them. On the ear wire, add one bicone in color A, one bicone in color B, and one crimp tube. Flatten the crimp tube to secure the beads to the ear wire.

TIP
You can replace the bicones with faceted ovals of the same size.

COMET RING

Materials

2 bicones, 6mm dia., color A (ochre)

4 bicones, 4mm dia., color A (ochre)

1 rectangular montée, 15mm long, color A (ochre)

4 rhinestone rondells, 6mm dia, color A (ochre)

6 bicones, 4mm dia., color B (peach)

11/0 rocailles, ochre

12 faceted ovals, ochre (for ring band)

40 in. (1.0m) beading thread

2 beading needles

Difficulty ★ ★ ★

1 On the center of the thread, string one 6mm bicone, one 4mm bicone in color A, one 4mm bicone in color B, and one 4mm bicone in color A. Cross through a 6mm bicone. (Avoid pulling the threads too tight.)

2 On each thread, string one 4mm bicone in color B and one rhinestone rondelle. Pass through the montée. To each thread, add one rhinestone rondelle and one 4mm bicone in color B. Cross through one 6mm bicone. On each thread, string one 4mm bicone in color A. Cross through one 4mm bicone in color B.

3 Pass each thread through the outside beads, adding rocailles where shown. Cross in a 4mm bicone. To begin the band, string on each thread two rocailles and one faceted oval. Continue the band with rocailles and faceted ovals. Join the threads, and knot them.

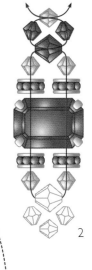

Materials

13 bicones, 6mm dia., color A (ochre)

6 bicones, 4mm dia., color A (ochre)

12 bicones, 6mm dia., color B (garnet)

42 bicones, 4mm dia., color B (garnet)

10 bicones, 6mm dia., color C (khaki)

24 bicones, 4mm dia., color C (khaki)

11/0 rocailles, ochre

2 jump rings and one lobster-claw clasp

2 lengths 24 gauge wire, each 32 in. (81.2cm), gold

Difficulty ★ ★ ★

Techniques: Clasps (See page 13.)
Jump Rings (See page 13.)
Assembling Picks (See page 17.)
The Square Cross (See page 20.)

ENCHANTED BRACELET

Note: This bracelet measures 6 in. (15.2cm) without findings.

1 Wrap the ends of both wires around the edge of a jump ring, allowing 1 in. (2.5cm) to extend. Pass both wires through one 4mm bicone in color C. On each wire, string one rocaille and one 4mm bicone in color C. Cross in one 6mm bicone in color A. Tuck the wire ends into the beads to conceal them.

2 Make the first flower. On each wire, string one 4mm bicone in color C. Cross in one 4mm bicone in color B. On each end, string one 4mm bicone in color C. Cross in one 6mm bicone in color A.

3 Begin the picks at the top and bottom of the bracelet. On one wire, string one 6mm bicone in color B and one rocaille. Pass through one bicone. Cross in one bicone. Repeat with the second wire.

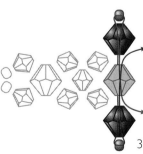

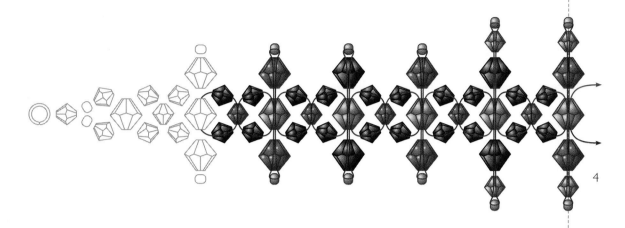

4

Make four more flowers as in step 2, using color B for the petals and color C for the centers. Add picks between each flower as in step 3, alternating bicone colors B and C. For the middle of the bracelet, make three flowers. For the picks, alternate 6mm bicones in colors B and C, and add 4mm bicones in color A at the ends as shown. Make four more flowers, using color B for the petals and color C for the centers.

Follow step 3 for the picks. Make one flower using color C for the petals and color B for the center. Cross in one 6mm bicone in color A. On each wire, string one 4mm bicone in color C and one rocaille. Pass together through one 4mm bicone in color C. Attach the wire to the jump ring as in step 1. Cut the ends to 1 in. (2.5cm). Tuck the wire ends into the beads to conceal them. Attach the clasp to the jump ring.

TIP

For a longer bracelet, add an additional flower at each end. The first and last picks should be in color C.

JENNIFER RING

Materials

12 flowers, 6mm dia., khaki

13 bicones, 4mm dia, khaki

11/0 rocailles, khaki

12 faceted ovals, khaki
(for ring band)

48 in. (1.2m) beading thread

2 beading needles

Difficulty ★ ★ ★

*Technique: The 4-Rose
(See page 21.)*

1 | On the thread, center one bicone, one rocaille, one bicone, one flower, one bicone, and one flower. Cross through the first bicone to make the first triangle of the rose.

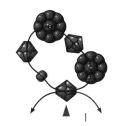

2 | On the right thread (red), string one flower, one bicone, and one flower. On the left thread (blue), string one rocaille. Cross through one bicone. Repeat once. On the left thread (red), string one flower. On the right thread (blue), string one rocaille. Pass through one bicone. Add one flower. Cross through one bicone.

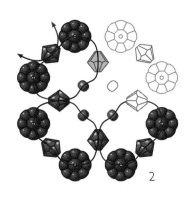

3 | Pass both threads through all the outside beads, placing one rocaille between each flower. Cross in one bicone.

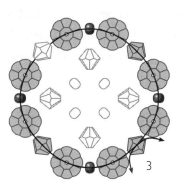

4 Pass each thread through four outside bicones. Add three rocailles, one flower, and three rocailles between each bicone as shown. Cross in one flower. On each thread, string one bicone. Cross through one bicone. Continue the band with the rocailles and faceted ovals. End symmetrically. Join the threads, and knot them.

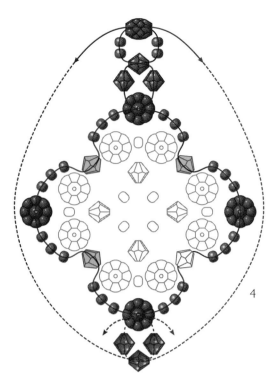

TIP
For a more whimsical design, use a different color for each one of the beads.

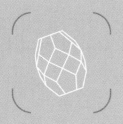

Materials

6 bicones, 6mm dia., color A
(pale pink)

2 bicones, 6mm dia., color B
(ochre)

4 bicones, 4mm dia., color B
(ochre)

8 faceted ovals, 4mm dia., color B
(ochre)

10 bicones, 4mm dia., color C
(pink)

6 bicones, 4mm dia., color D
(fuchsia)

11/0 rocailles, yellow

12 faceted ovals, yellow
(for ring band)

52 in. (1.3m) beading thread

2 beading needles

Difficulty ★ ★ ★

*Technique: The Square Cross
(See page 20.)*

LARK RING

1 | Make a row of five squares as shown. For the first and fifth squares, string one faceted oval, two 4mm bicones in color C, and one 4mm bicone in color D. For the second and fourth squares, string two 4mm bicones in color B and one 6mm bicone in color A. For the third square, string two 6mm bicones in color B. Cross in the last faceted oval.

2 | Pass each thread through one bicone. Add one rocaille. Pass through one bicone.

3 | On each thread, string one rocaille, one 6mm bicone in color A, one faceted oval, and one 4mm bicone in color C. Pass through one rocaille, one bicone, one rocaille, and one 6mm bicone as shown.

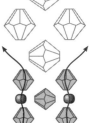

4 On each thread, string one rocaille, one 6mm bicone in color A, and one faceted oval. Pass through one 6mm bicone, one rocaille, one 6mm bicone, one rocaille, and one 4mm bicone.

5 On each thread, string one rocaille, one 4mm bicone in color C, and one faceted oval. Pass through one 6mm bicone, one rocaille, one 6mm bicone, one rocaille, and one 4mm bicone. Cross in a faceted oval.

6 Pass each thread through all the outside faceted ovals, adding the rocailles as shown. Begin the band as shown. Continue with the rocailles and faceted ovals. End symmetrically. Join the threads, and knot them.

TIP

It is the variety of vivid colors that contributes to the originality of this design. Feel free to substitute softer colors.

NORA RING

Materials

1 maquise montée, 15mm long, color A (mauve)

6 bicones, 4mm dia., color A (mauve)

6 bicones, 4mm dia., color B (fuchsia)

2 bicones, 6mm dia., color C (ochre)

2 marquise montées, 10mm long, color D (violet)

11/0 rocailles, gold

12 faceted ovals, fuchsia (for ring band)

40 in. (1.0m) beading thread

2 beading needles

Difficulty ★ ★ ★

I On the thread, center one rocaille. Pass both threads through one 4mm bicone in color A. On each thread, add one rocaille. Pass the threads through the top and bottom holes of one 10mm montée. On each thread, add two rocailles, one 4mm bicone in color B, one rocaille, one 6mm bicone, and two rocailles. Pass each through a 15mm montée from the bottom to the top. Add two rocailles. Pass in a 6mm bicone.

2 Referring to the diagram, use the left thread (red) to string the same pattern of beads. Cross in the right 6mm bicone. Pass the right thread (blue) around the assembly. Cross in the right 6mm bicone.

3 Begin the band as shown. Continue with the rocailles and faceted ovals. End symmetrically. Join the threads, and knot them.

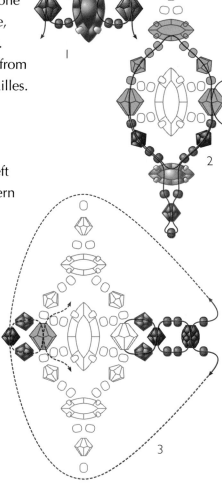

Winter

Even if cold winds blow and snow covers your front steps, you can warm up your wardrobe with colorful jewlery in hot colors and deep shades that reveal their splendor by the light of a fire.

At holiday time, dress up an ensemble with the "Declaration" set; add mystery with the "Midnight" ring; and accent your décolletage with the "Evening-Party" pendant. They all add brilliant sparkle to the long winter night.

TREASURED SET

Earring materials

8 pearls, 6mm dia., color A (off white)

4 bicones, 6mm dia., color B (light brown)

6 bicones, 4mm dia., color C (crystal)

11/0 rocailles, gold

Hook ear wires, gold

2 strands beading thread, each 16 in. (40.6cm)

2 beading needles

Difficulty ★ ★ ★

*Techniques: Assembling Picks
(See page 17.)
The Square Cross (See page 20.)*

Earrings

1 Make two earrings. Have the center of the thread in the ring of the ear wire. On each thread, string three rocailles. Pass both ends through one 6mm bicone. On each end, string four pearls. Cross in the bottom right pearl.

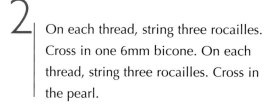

2 On each thread, string three rocailles. Cross in one 6mm bicone. On each thread, string three rocailles. Cross in the pearl.

3 On the left thread (blue), string one 4mm bicone and one rocaille. Pass through the bicone and the pearl to make the first pick. Repeat twice. Knot the threads; insert them through the top 6mm bicone, and cut the end.

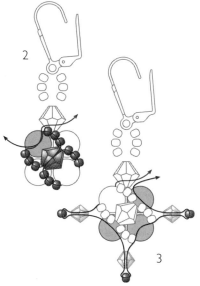

TIP
To give this design more volume, replace the 4mm bicones on the picks with 6mm bicones.

Pendant

1 Make a "carpet" using 18 pearls.

2 On each thread, string one 4mm bicone. Cross in one 6mm bicone. On each thread, string one 4mm bicone. Cross in the pearl. Repeat. Pass the left thread (blue) through one rocaille, one pearl, one rocaille, and one pearl. String one 4mm bicone, one 6mm bicone, and one 4mm bicone. Cross in the pearl. Repeat three times.

3 Pass the right thread (red) through one rocaille and one pearl. Repeat four times. String one 4mm bicone. Pass in the 6mm bicone. Add one 4mm bicone. Repeat three times. Cross in the pearl. Add one rocaille. Cross in the pearl.

4 On the top thread (blue), string one rocaille. Pass in the pearl. String one rocaille. Pass in the pearl. On the bottom thread (red), string one rocaille. Complete the carpet as shown.

5 Refer to the diagram, and add the remaining 4mm and 6mm bicones. Cross the threads in the pearls as shown.

6 On each thread, string one rocaille. Cross in the pearls. Add one rocaille at the center. Follow the diagram for the loop. Pass through the beads to join the threads, and knot them.

Pendant materials

23 pearls, 6mm dia., color A (off white)

9 bicones, 6mm dia., color B (light brown)

32 bicones, 4mm dia., color C (crystal)

11/0 rocailles, gold

Hanging ribbon or cord with findings as desired

40 in. (1.0m) beading thread

2 beading needles

Difficulty ★ ★ ★

Technique: The Square Cross (See page 20.)

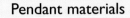

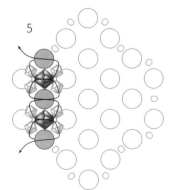

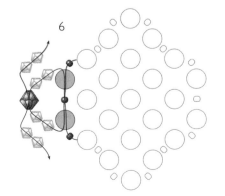

TREASURED SET

Ring materials

23 pearls, 6mm dia., color A
(off white)

8 bicones, 6mm dia., color B
(light brown)

6 bicones, 4mm dia., color C
(crystal)

11/0 rocailles, gold

12 faceted ovals, crystal
(for ring band)

48 in. (1.2m) beading thread

2 beading needles

Difficulty ★ ★ ★

*Technique: The Square Cross
(See page 20.)*

Ring

1 | Follow step 1 of the pendant on page 137 to assemble the carpet. Also refer to step 2 of the pendant, substituting four rocailles for each 4mm bicone.

2 | Pass the right thread (red) through one rocaille and one pearl. Repeat five times. String one 4mm bicone. Pass in the pearl. Repeat twice. On the left thread (blue), string three rocailles. Pass in the 6mm bicone. String three rocailles. Pass in a pearl. Repeat three times. Add one rocaille. Cross in the bottom left pearl.

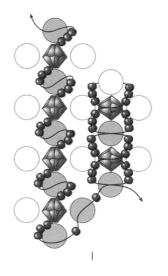

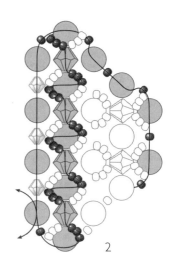

3

On the bottom thread (red), pass in one rocaille, one pearl, one rocaille, and one pearl. Add one 4mm bicone; pass in the pearl. Repeat twice. Pass in one rocaille, one pearl, one rocaille, and one pearl. Add one rocaille and three pearls. Pass in one pearl. Add one pearl. On the top thread (blue), add one rocaille. Following the diagram, pass through five pearls.

4

To the thread (blue), add three rocailles, one 6mm bicone in color B, and three rocailles. Pass in the pearl. Add three rocailles, one 6mm bicone, and three rocailles. Pass in the pearl. Add one rocaille. Pass in the pearl. Add one rocaille. Pass in the pearl. Add five rocailles, one oval, two rocailles, and one oval. To the thread (red), add three rocailles. Pass in the 6mm bicone in color B. Add three rocailles. Pass in the pearl. Add three rocailles. Pass in the 6mm bicone. Add three rocailles. Pass in the pearl. Add one rocaille. Pass in the pearl, one rocaille, and one pearl. Add five rocailles. Pass in the oval. Add two rocailles. Pass in the oval. Refer to page 18 to make the band, beginning with the rocailles and the ovals. End symmetrically. Join the threads, and knot them.

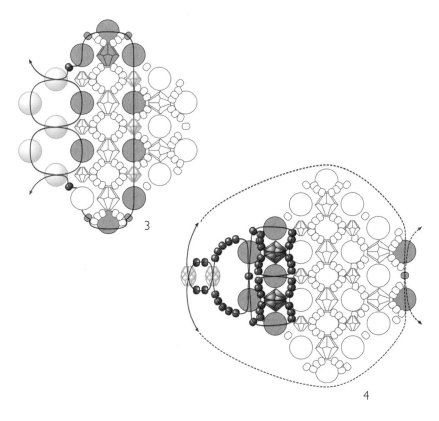

COUNTESS RING

Materials

1 rectangular montée, 15mm long, color A (burgundy)

14 bicones, 4mm dia., color A (burgundy)

9 bicones, 4mm dia., color B (red)

32 bicones, 4mm, color C (dark burgundy)

11/0 rocailles, red

12 faceted ovals, red (for ring band)

60 in. (1.5m) beading thread

2 beading needles

Difficulty

1 | On the thread, center four rocailles. Cross through the montée. On each thread, string 10 rocailles.

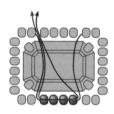

1

2 | Cross both threads through the montée. Cross through five rocailles. Pass the threads together through the montée.

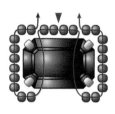

2

3 | Pass the left thread (red) to the left through one rocaille. Add one bicone in color A, one rocaille, one bicone in color C, one rocaille, and one bicone in color A. Cross through the same rocaille. Pass left through four rocailles. Repeat five times. Pass the right thread (blue) to the right through four rocailles. On each thread (as indicated by the arrow), string one bicone in color A and one rocaille. Cross through one bicone in color C.

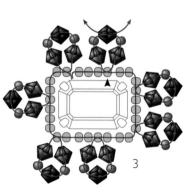

3

4 Turn the assembly face down. On the right thread (blue), string one rocaille, one bicone in color B, and one rocaille. Pass through the beads of the triangle. Repeat five times. String one rocaille, one bicone in color B, and one rocaille. Pass through one rocaille and one bicone.

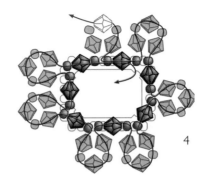

5 On the bottom thread (blue), string one rocaille, one bicone in color C, and one rocaille. Pass in the following bicone. Repeat six times. Pass through the following bicone.

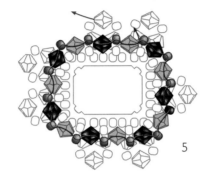

6 Turn the assembly face up. On the right thread (red), string one rocaille. Pass in a bicone at the tip of the next triangle. Repeat six times. Pass in the next bicone.

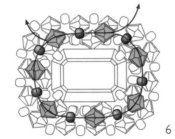

7 To begin the border, pass the right thread (red) in one rocaille at the left. String one rocaille, one bicone in color C, and one rocaille. Pass in a rocaille. Repeat 13 times, passing in one rocaille at the top. At the bottom, alternate between passing in one rocaille and one bicone as shown.

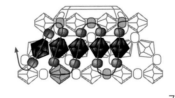

TIP

This design is equally stunning when worked in all emerald or all blue sapphire beads.

8 Pass both threads through several beads so that they cross in the middle bicone on the long side of the montée. Refer to page 18 to make the band, beginning as shown; then continue with the rocailles and ovals. End symmetrically. Join the threads, and knot them.

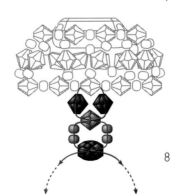

EVENING-PARTY PENDANT

Materials

1 rectangular montée, 15mm long, color A (crystal)

5 marquise montées, 10mm long, color A (crystal)

4 marquise montées, 15mm long, color B (blue)

38 bicones, 4mm dia., color B (blue)

11/0 rocailles, crystal

Hanging ribbon or cord with findings as desired

40 in. (1.0m) beading thread

2 beading needles

Difficulty ★ ★ ★

1 Note: String the montées through the lower holes in this step. On the thread, string one 15mm marquise montée in color B, one bicone, one 10mm marquise montée in color A, and 1 bicone. Repeat three times. Cross the threads in the first 15mm montée. Pull the threads tight. Have the thread ends even.

2 Note: String the montées through the upper holes in this step. On the right thread (blue), string two bicones. Pass in the montées. Repeat twice. String two bicones. Cross in the bottom 15mm montée. Repeat with the left thread (red).

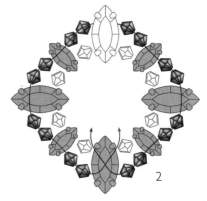

3 Pass each thread through the bicones and lower holes of the montées. Cross in the top 15mm montée. Pass through the bicones and upper holes of the montées. Cross in the bottom 15mm montée.

4   On each thread, string one bicone. Pass through the rectangular montée. String one bicone on each thread. Cross through the lower holes of the top marquise montée. Pass through the beads and lower holes of the marquise montées as shown.

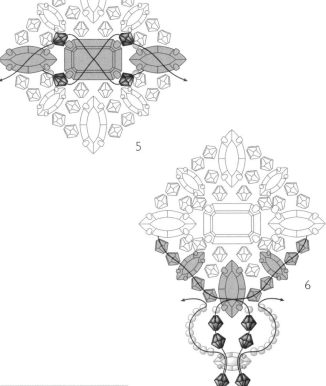

5   On each thread, string one rocaille and one bicone. Cross in the rectangular montée. On each thread, string one bicone and one rocaille. Pass in the marquise montées.

6   Pass the threads through the bicones and the upper holes of the marquise montées. Cross in the upper holes of the bottom marquise montée. For the loop, string one rocaille and two bicones on each thread. Pass in one 10mm marquise montée. On each thread, string one bicone and one rocaille. Pass through the bicones and the 10mm marquise montée. String nine rocailles on each thread. Cross in the bottom marquise montée. Pass in the beads to join the threads, and knot them.

4

5

6

TIP
Be sure the threads pass and cross through the holes in the montées as shown in the diagrams.

KNIGHT'S RING

Materials

5 rhinestone rondelles, 4mm dia., crystal

30 bicones, 4mm dia., crystal

4 cubes, 4mm dia., crystal

11/0 rocailles, crystal

12 faceted ovals, crystal (for ring band)

60 in. (1.5m) beading thread

2 beading needles

Difficulty ★ ★ ★

1
On the thread, string six rocailles. Cross through two bicones. Center the beads on the thread so that the ends are even. On each end, string one rocaille. Cross through three bicones. On each end, string one rocaille. Cross through four bicones. On each thread, string one rocaille. Cross through one bicone, one rhinestone rondelle, one cube, one rhinestone rondelle, and one bicone. On each thread, string one rocaille. Cross through one bicone, one cube, one rhinestone rondelle, one cube, and one bicone. Repeat the first three rows, working in reverse. End by crossing through two bicones.

2
Pass the left thread (red) through one rocaille. String one rocaille. Repeat twice. Pass through one rocaille. String one bicone and one rocaille. Pass through the bicone and one rocaille. String one rocaille. Pass through one rocaille. Repeat with the right thread (blue).

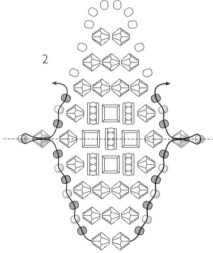

3 On the left thread (red), string one rocaille and one bicone. Pass through one rocaille. String one bicone and one rocaille. Pass through three rocailles. String one rocaille. Pass through three rocailles. String one rocaille. Pass through one rocaille. String one rocaille. Pass through one rocaille. Repeat with the right thread (blue). On the left thread, string two bicones and four rocailles. On the right thread (red), cross through both bicones. String two rocailles. Cross through two rocailles.

4 Refer to page 18 to make the band, stringing it with one rocaille between each faceted oval. End symmetrically. Join the threads, and knot them.

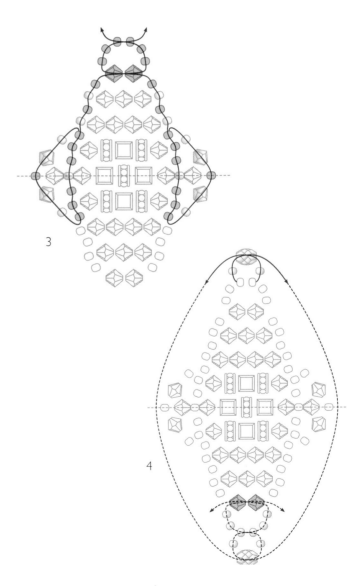

TIP

It is essential to hold the threads tight after assembling each row.

SHOOTING-STAR SET

Ring materials

16 faceted ovals, 4mm dia., color A (burgundy)

18 bicones, 4mm dia., color A (burgundy)

8 bicones, 4mm dia., color B (white opal)

16 bicones, 4mm dia., color C (light brown)

1 round montée, 6mm dia., color C (light brown)

11/0 rocailles, light brown

12 faceted ovals, burgundy (for ring band)

48 in. (1.2m) beading thread

2 beading needles

Difficulty ★ ★ ★

Ring

1 On the thread, center 12 faceted ovals. Pass the thread again through all of the beads. Cross in the first oval.

2 On the right thread (red), string one bicone in color A, one bicone in color B, and one bicone in color A. Cross through the next two faceted ovals at the right. Repeat five times. Cross through the next faceted oval.

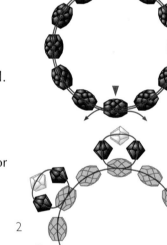

3 Pass the left thread (blue) through one bicone. String one bicone in color C, one bicone in color A, and one bicone in color C. Pass through one bicone and one faceted oval. Repeat five times. End by passing through one bicone.

4 Pass the left thread (red) in three bicones. String one rocaille. Pass in one bicone. Repeat around the outside as shown. Cross in the first bicone at the bottom left. Pass the right thread (blue) in two faceted ovals and three bicones. Pass in the rocailles and bicones around the outside. Cross in the bottom left bicone.

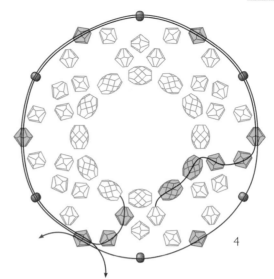

4

5 Tighten the thread to form the assembly into a dome shape. (The faceted ovals are now under the bicones.) Pass both threads from the top of the ring down, and pass through the middle bicones. On each thread, string one faceted oval. Pass each through the montée. String one faceted oval on each. Pass each through two bicones. Refer to page 18 to make the band, beginning it by crossing in the faceted oval. On each thread, add one bicone in color C. Pass in one bicone in color B. Add two rocailles, and cross in a faceted oval. End symmetrically. Join the threads, and knot them.

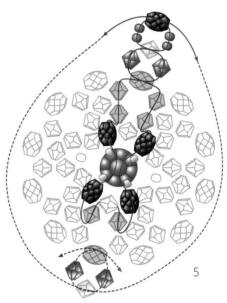

5

Pendant materials

1 bicone, 6mm dia., color A (burgundy)

7 bicones, 4mm dia., color A (burgundy)

6 bicones, 4mm dia., color B (white opal)

44 bicones, 4mm dia., color C (light brown)

Hanging ribbon or cord with findings as desired

11/0 rocailles, light brown

40 in. (1.0m) beading thread

2 beading needles

Difficulty ★ ★ ★

Variation materials

1 bicone, 6mm dia., color A (light brown)

30 bicones, 4mm dia., color A (light brown)

30 bicones, 4mm dia., color B (gold)

11/0 rocailles, gold

Hanging ribbon or cord with findings as desired

40 in. (1.0m) beading thread

2 beading needles

Pendant

1 Center 12 4mm bicones in color C on the thread. Cross in the first bicone.

2 Follow steps 2 and 3 of the ring on page 146. (Note the color placement.) Pass the threads to exit the same way as step 3 of the ring. Pass the right thread (blue) to the left through the bicones. Cross in the bottom right bicone. Pass the left thread (red) to cross in the same bicone as the blue thread. On each end, string one 4mm bicone in color C. Cross in a 6mm bicone. On each thread, string one 4mm bicone in color C. Cross and pass in the bicones as shown. String the beads for the loop as shown. Cross in one 4mm bicone in color B. Pass the threads through the beads, and knot them.

Variation

1 | Follow steps 1 and 2 of the pendant on page 148. (Do not make the loop.) Pass the left thread (blue) in four bicones. String two rocailles, one 4mm bicone in color A, two rocailles, one 4mm bicone in color B, and two rocailles. Pass in one bicone. String two rocailles. Cross in the bicone. String four rocailles. Cross in a bicone. Pass in the bicones. Repeat with the right thread (red), working toward the right. Cross the threads in one bicone.

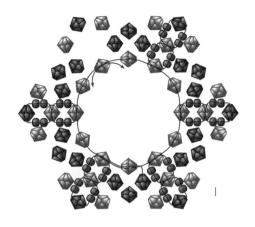

2 | On each thread, string one bicone in color B. Pass together through the 6mm bicone in color A and one rocaille. Pass together through the 6mm bicone. Pass each thread through the bicones. For the loop, see step 2 on page 148.

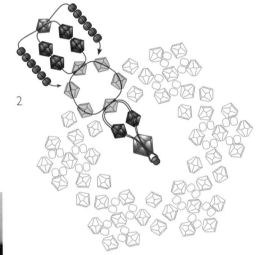

> **TIP**
> *For this variation, a tear drop could be used in place of the 6mm bicone.*

OVAL RING

Materials

26 bicones, 4mm dia., color A (gold)

26 faceted ovals, 4mm dia., color B (fuchsia)

32 bicones, 4mm dia., color B (fuchsia)

11/0 rocailles, gold

12 faceted ovals, gold (for ring band)

60 in. (1.5m) beading thread

2 beading needles

Difficulty ★ ★ ★

Technique: The Square Cross (See page 20.)

1 | Use the faceted ovals to make one column of three squares. Cross in the beginning oval. Use both threads to make the bicone flowers. On each thread, string one bicone in color B and one in color A. Cross in one rocaille. On each thread, string one bicone in color A and one in color B. Cross in the faceted oval. Repeat twice.

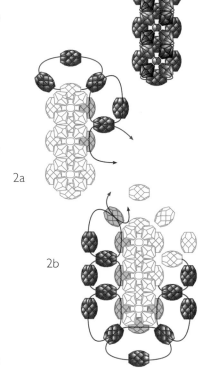

2a

2b

2 | On the left thread (red), string three faceted ovals. Cross the right thread (blue) in the last oval strung. Add two faceted ovals to the right thread. Pass the left thread (red) through one faceted oval; then cross in one oval. Repeat around the column, following diagrams 2a and 2b. End by crossing in the top left faceted oval.

3 | Start at the top and work clockwise, following the diagram. As in step 1, use both threads to make the bicone flowers over the outside row of faceted ovals. Cross the threads in the beginning oval.

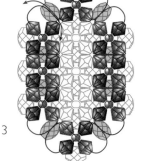

3

4

Pass the left thread (red) through the outside bicones, and tighten it to form a dome shape. Cross through the top faceted oval.

5

Pass the right thread (blue) in the bottom two bicones of the top flower. To the same thread, add one bicone in color B. Pass in two bicones. Repeat around the assembly. Pass diagonally in one bicone, one rocaille, and one bicone of the top flower. Cross in the top oval.

6

Pass both threads around the assembly to cross in the oval at the right. Refer to page 18, beginning the band as shown. Continue with the rocailles and ovals. End symmetrically. Join the threads, and knot them.

TIP

This design has the most impact when dark-colored bicones are used in step 5.

DECLARATION SET

Materials

1 bicone, 6mm dia., color A (crystal)

1 rhinestone rondelle, 4mm dia., color A (crystal)

99 bicones, 4mm dia., color A (crystal)

21 bicones, 4 mm dia., color B (iridescent black)

Hanging ribbon or cord with findings as desired

11/0 rocailles, crystal

80 in. (2.0m) beading thread

2 beading needles

Difficulty ★ ★ ★

Technique: The Square Cross (See page 20.)

Pendant

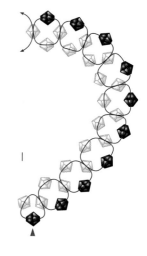

1 On the thread, center one bicone in color B and two bicones in color A. Cross in the last bicone to make one triangle. On the right thread (blue), string one bicone in color B. On the left thread (red), string two bicones in color A. Cross in one bicone in color A to complete one square. Make nine squares.

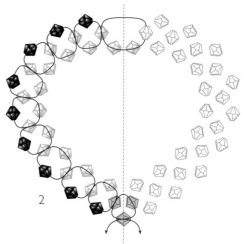

2 On the bottom thread (blue), string three bicones in color A. Cross the top thread (red) through the last bicone. Make eight squares as in step 1. For the ninth square, on the bottom thread (blue), string one bicone in color B. On the top thread (red), string one bicone in color A. Cross the threads in the bicone of the triangle. Pass and cross the threads in the triangle.

3 String one bicone in color A on each thread. Cross through the bicone on the right to make one triangle. Pass the top thread (blue) in one bicone. On the bottom thread (red), string two bicones in color A. Cross the top thread in one bicone in color A to complete one square. Make nine squares. On the top thread (blue), string three bicones in color A. Cross through one bicone. Make nine squares as shown. Cross in the bottom left bicone.

4 Pass and cross both threads through the bicones as shown, adding one 4mm bicone in color A between each row of two bicones. Tighten the threads. (This will draw the edges closer and give the heart dimension. Once the threads are tightened, the color B bicones will be along the outside edge of the heart.)

5 Pass both threads through all of the bicones to the top of the heart. For the loop, string one 4mm bicone in color B, one rhinestone rondelle, and one 4mm bicone in color B on both threads. On each thread, string four rocailles. Cross in the 6mm bicone. Add four rocailles to each thread. Join the threads, and knot them.

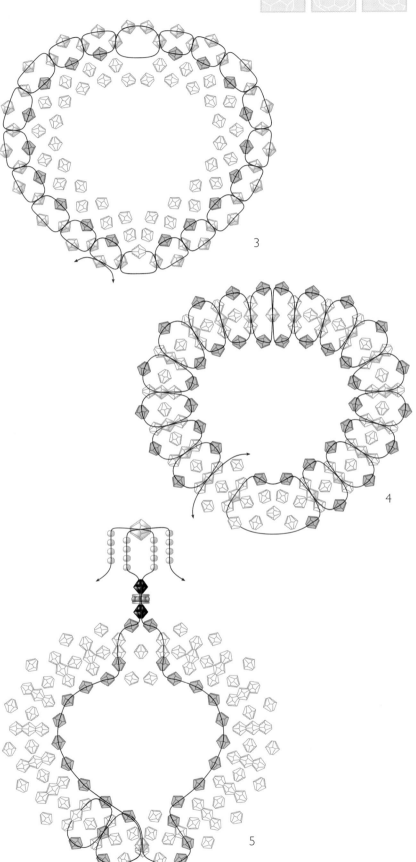

DECLARATION SET

Bracelet materials

84 faceted ovals, 4mm, color A (crystal)

60 bicones, 4mm dia., color A (crystal)

60 bicones, 4mm dia., color B (iridescent black)

11/0 rocailles, crystal

2 bead tips, 2 jump rings, and 1 lobster-claw clasp, gold

2 strands beading thread, each 60 in. (1.5m)

2 beading needles

Difficulty ★ ★ ★

Techniques: Bead Tips (See page 12.) Clasps (See page 13.) Jump rings (See page 13.) The Square Cross (See page 20.)

Bracelet

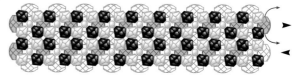

1. Use one strand and the faceted ovals to make two rows of nine squares. Cross in the bottom right faceted oval.

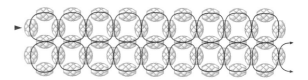

2. Make the bottom row of the bicone flower first; then make the top row. Alternate the bicone colors for the petals as shown. Cross in one rocaille at the center of the flower. Cross in the following faceted oval.

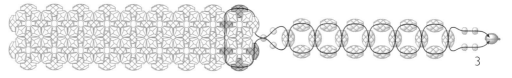

3. Pass the top thread (red) through the faceted ovals. Pass both threads through one rocaille. On each thread, string one rocaille. Use faceted ovals to make six squares. Cross in the right oval. On each thread, string two rocailles. Pass both threads through the bead tip. Cross in one rocaille. Make a knot close to the rocaille. Trim the threads, and close the bead tip.

4

4

Pass the second strand of the thread through the left faceted oval at the arrow. Make six flowers. Cross in the right oval.

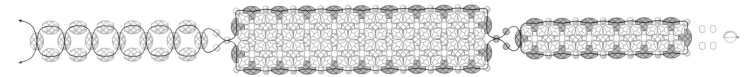

5

5

Pass both threads in the outside faceted ovals, stringing one rocaille between each. Pass in the rocailles between the right sections. Pass in the left ovals. On both threads, string one rocaille. On each thread, string one rocaille. Use faceted ovals to make a row of six squares as in step 3.

6

6

Make six flowers as in step 4. Cross in the right oval. Pass each thread through the outside faceted ovals, stringing one rocaille between each. Cross in the left oval. On each thread, string two rocailles. Pass both threads through the bead tip. String one rocaille on both threads. Make a knot close to the rocaille. Trim the threads, and close the bead tip. Secure the jump ring and the clasp at one end. Secure a jump ring at the other end.

TIP

It is easy to adjust the length of this bracelet by adding or subtracting as many squares as necessary.

FUCHSIA SET

Earring materials

8 bicones, 4mm dia., color A (purple)

2 buttons, 10mm dia., color A (purple)

16 bicones, 4mm dia., color B (mauve)

8 faceted ovals, 4mm dia., color C (violet)

11/0 rocailles, violet

Hook ear wires, silver

2 strands beading thread, each 20 in. (50.8cm)

2 beading needles

Difficulty ★ ★ ★

Earrings

1 Make two earrings. Have the center of the thread in the ring of the ear wire. On each thread, string two rocailles. Cross both ends through the faceted oval. On each thread, string one faceted oval. Cross in one faceted oval.

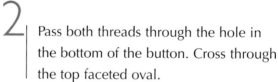

2 Pass both threads through the hole in the bottom of the button. Cross through the top faceted oval.

3 On the right thread (blue), string one rocaille, one bicone in color B, one bicone in color A, one bicone in color B, and one rocaille. Cross through the same faceted oval. Pass through the faceted oval at the left. Repeat three times. Cross in the top faceted oval.

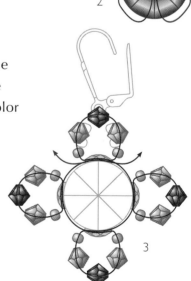

4

Pass the left thread (red) through one rocaille and two bicones. Pass the thread around the ear wire, and cross through the bicone. Pass in one bicone and one rocaille. Knot the ends.

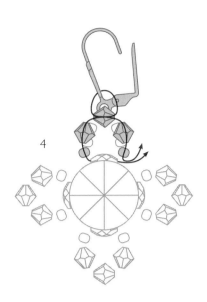

Pendant materials

9 bicones, 4mm dia., color A (purple)

1 button, 10mm dia., color B (purple)

1 faceted square, 20mm x 20mm, color A (purple)

16 bicones, 4mm dia., color B (mauve)

4 faceted ovals, 4mm dia., color C (violet)

1 bicone, 6mm dia., color C (blue)

Hanging ribbon or cord with findings as desired

11/0 rocailles, violet

40 in. (1.0m) beading thread

2 beading needles

Difficulty ★ ★ ★

Pendant

Center four faceted ovals on the thread. Cross the thread in the bottom oval. On the left thread (blue), string one rocaille, one bicone in color B, one bicone in color A, one bicone in color B, and one rocaille. Cross in the same oval. Pass to the right through one oval. Repeat the assembly once. Cross in the top oval. On the right thread (red), pass to the left through one oval. Repeat the assembly. Cross in the top oval, and repeat the assembly. Cross in the top oval.

2 Pass both threads through the hole in the bottom of the button. Cross through the bottom faceted oval.

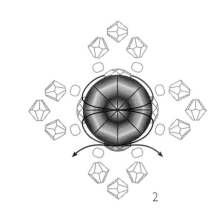

2

3 On each thread, string eight rocailles and two bicones in color A. Place the faceted square behind the assembly. Cross the threads in the bottom bicone of the assembly. (The rocailles will be on the wrong side of the square.)

4 Pass both threads through two 4mm bicones. To begin the loop, cross in the 6mm bicone. On each thread, string two bicones in color B. Cross in one bicone in color A. On each thread, string two bicones in color B. Pass each thread through one bicone. Cross the threads in the bottom bicone of the assembly. Pass the threads through the bicones and the rocailles on the front of the assembly. Cross in one faceted oval. Pass them together through the button, and knot them.

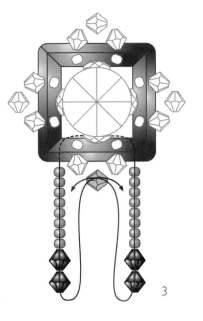

3

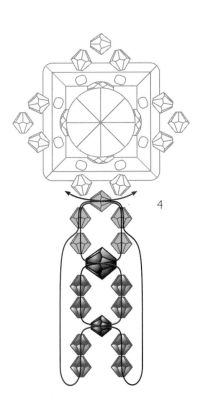

4

TIP

You can make the points longer (except the one supporting the loop) by stringing five bicones instead of three. This will add more volume to the pendant.

PLANET RING

Materials

24 bicones, 4mm dia., color A
(blue)

28 faceted ovals, 4mm dia.,
color A (blue)

32 bicones, 4mm dia., color B
(blue gray)

11/0 rocailles, blue

12 faceted ovals, blue
(for ring band)

56 in. (1.4m) beading thread

2 beading needles

Difficulty ★ ★ ★

*Technique: The Square Cross
(See page 20.)*

1 | Use the faceted ovals to make a "carpet"
of four squares. Cross in the bottom right
oval. Use both threads to make the
flowers using bicones in colors A and B
(for the petals) and the rocaille (for the
center). Cross in the top left oval.

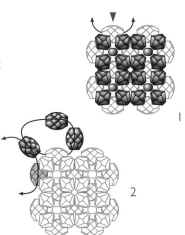

2 | On the right thread (blue), string three
faceted ovals. Pass in the oval. Cross
the left thread (red) in the faceted oval.

3 | Work counterclockwise. On the left
thread, string two faceted ovals. Cross
in the faceted oval. Pass the right
thread through one oval. String two
ovals. Cross in the oval. Repeat around
the carpet. Cross in the oval at the top.

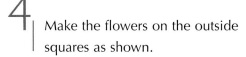

4 | Make the flowers on the outside
squares as shown.

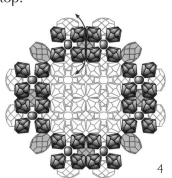

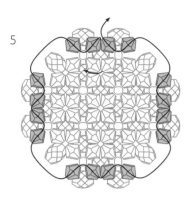

5

Pass the top thread (blue) in the outside bicones. Tighten to make a dome shape. Pass both threads in the bicones.

6

Pass the top thread (blue) in the outside faceted ovals. Pass in the top right oval. Pass the bottom thread (red) in the bicones.

7

On the left thread (red), string one bicone in color B. Pass through two bicones of the flower. Repeat. Cross in the top right oval. Refer to page 18 to make the band, using rocailles and ovals. End symmetrically. Join the threads, and knot them.

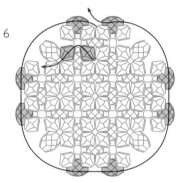

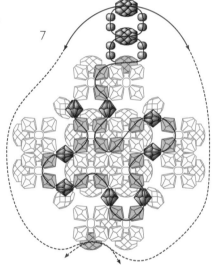

TIP

For a larger ring for the most formal events, change the design by using 6mm faceted ovals and bicones in crystal.

Pendant materials

12 bicones, 6mm dia., color A (burgundy)

13 bicones, 4mm dia., color A (burgundy)

6 bicones, 6mm dia., color B (dark red)

11 bicones, 4mm dia., color B (dark red)

Hanging ribbon or cord with findings as desired

1 antiqued round-filigree finding, 60mm dia.

11/0 rocailles, gold

3 strands beading thread: 1 strand, 60 in. (1.5m); other 2 strands, each 20 in. (50.8cm)

2 beading needles

Difficulty ★ ★ ★

Pendant

1 (Dashed lines on the diagram indicate threads on the back of the finding.) Insert the thread ends from the back of the finding through the holes where indicated. Have the thread ends even. On each thread, string one 6mm bicone in color A and one rocaille. Pass them together in one 6mm bicone in color B. On each thread, string one 6mm bicone in color A and one rocaille. Pass on the back to the holes indicated.

2 On each thread, string one rocaille, one 6mm bicone in color B, one rocaille, and one 4mm bicone in color A. Pass on the back to the holes indicated. On the left thread (blue), string one rocaille and one 4mm bicone in color A. Pass on the back. String one 4mm bicone in color B and one rocaille. Pass on the back. Repeat twice. On the right thread (red), string one rocaille and one 4mm bicone in color B. Pass on the back. String one 4mm bicone in color A and one rocaille. Pass on the back. Repeat twice. Pass both ends on the back to the center bottom of the finding.

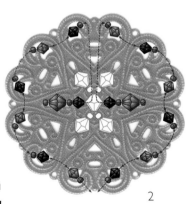

3

Cross the threads in one 6mm bicone in color A. On each thread, string one rocaille, one 4mm bicone in color A or B as shown, and one rocaille. Pass both threads through one 6mm bicone in color B, one rocaille, two 6mm bicones in color A, and one rocaille. Pass together through two 6mm bicones, one rocaille, and one 6mm bicone. Pass each thread through one rocaille, one 4mm bicone, and one rocaille. Cross in a 6mm bicone at the bottom of the finding. (This completes the pick.) Pass the left thread (blue) on the back. Pass through one rocaille. Bring to the front at the black arrow (See the diagram). String one 6mm bicone in color A. Pass in one rocaille. Pass on the back. Repeat to the top of the finding. Pass the thread to the front of the finding. Repeat with the right thread (red). For the loop, string one rocaille and two 4mm bicones in color A or B as shown. Cross in one 6mm bicone in color A. Add six rocailles to each thread. Pass the threads from the back of the finding to the front through the same holes. Pass through one rocaille and one bicone at the top left and right. Pass the threads to the back. Join the threads, and make a knot.

4

To begin the first pick, insert the ends of a 20 in. (50.8cm) length of thread from the back of the finding on either side of the bottom right hole. Have the thread ends even. With the ends together, string one rocaille, one 4mm bicone in color A, one rocaille, one 4mm bicone in color B, one rocaille, one 6mm bicone in color B, and one rocaille. To complete the pick, pass both threads back through all of the beads except the last rocaille strung. Pass the threads to the back, and knot them. Repeat for the left pick.

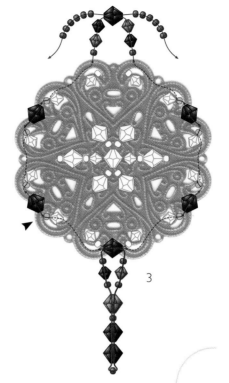

3

TIP

To ensure that the beads are secure on the finding, don't hesitate to pass the threads through all of the beads again. Then bring the ends to the back of the finding, and knot them.

ATTENTION

Dashed lines on the diagrams show where threads are on the back of the finding.

Earrings

Earring materials

10 bicones, 6mm dia., color A (burgundy)

14 bicones, 4mm dia., color A (burgundy)

10 bicones, 6mm dia., color B (dark red)

14 bicones, 4mm dia., color B (dark red)

11/0 rocailles, gold

Hook ear wires, antiqued gold

2 antiqued square-filigree findings, 20mm x 20mm

4 strands beading thread: 1 strand, 60 in. (1.5m); and 3 strands, each 16 in. (40cm)

2 beading needles

Difficulty ★ ★ ★

1 | Make two earrings. (Dashed lines on the diagram indicate the threads on the back of the finding.) Starting at the arrow, make the center motif as in steps 1 and 2 of the pendant on page 162. Bring each thread end to the back as shown by the red and blue arrows.

2 | Bring the threads to the front. On each thread, string one 4mm bicone in color B, one rocaille, and one 4mm bicone in color B. Bring the threads to the back through the closest hole. Join the threads, and knot them. Using 16-in. (15.2cm) strands of thread, make three picks as described in step 4 of the pendant on page 163. Follow the diagram for bead color and size.

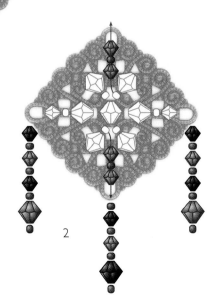

OCEAN RING

Materials

4 bicones, 6mm dia., color A (blue)

4 oval beads, 6mm dia., color A (blue)

14 bicones, 4mm dia., color B (dark blue)

4 round montées, 4mm dia., color C (gray)

11/0 rocailles, blue

12 faceted ovals, blue (for ring band)

56 in. (1.4m) beading thread

2 beading needles

Difficulty ★ ★ ★

Technique: The 4-Rose (See page 22.)

1 On the center of the thread, string one oval, one rocaille, one 6mm bicone, one rocaille, one oval, and one 4mm bicone. Cross in the first oval to complete the first triangle.

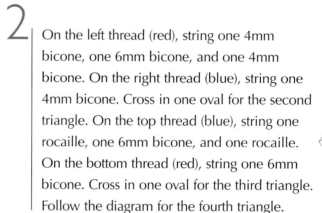

2 On the left thread (red), string one 4mm bicone, one 6mm bicone, and one 4mm bicone. On the right thread (blue), string one 4mm bicone. Cross in one oval for the second triangle. On the top thread (blue), string one rocaille, one 6mm bicone, and one rocaille. On the bottom thread (red), string one 6mm bicone. Cross in one oval for the third triangle. Follow the diagram for the fourth triangle.

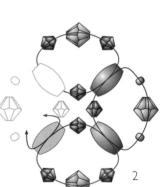

3 On the left thread (blue), string two rocailles, one montée, and one rocaille. Cross in the oval. On the right thread (red), add one rocaille. Cross in the montée. Add two rocailles. Cross in the oval. On the top thread (blue), string three rocailles, one montée, and two rocailles. Cross in the oval. On the bottom thread (red), string two rocailles. Cross in the montée. Add three rocailles. Cross in the oval. Repeat the pattern, and cross the threads as shown.

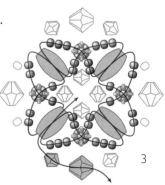

4

On both threads, string one rocaille. Pass the beads, and add the rocailles as shown. Cross in the 6mm bicone at the left. Refer to page 18 to make the band, beginning it as shown. Continue with the rocailles and faceted ovals. End symmetrically. Join the threads, and knot them.

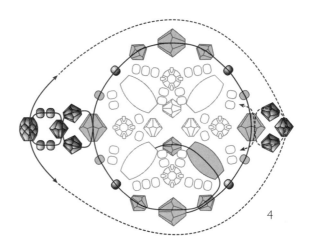

Variation

1

This variation is less dome-shaped than the original because of the beads used. Follow the assembly of the original design. Replace each oval with two 4mm faceted ovals. Substitute 4mm bicones for most of the rocailles following the diagram.

2

Follow step 3, replacing some rocailles with the 4mm bicones. Pass the beads, and add the rocailles as shown. Cross in a 6mm bicone at the top. Refer to page 18 to make the band. Begin as shown, then continue with the rocailles and ovals. Join the threads, and knot them.

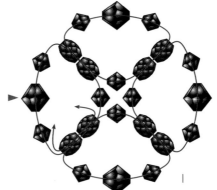

TIP

The height of the ring depends on the length of the oval beads.

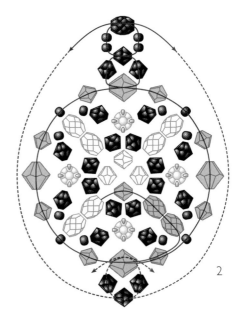

IMMORTAL RING

Materials

1 marquise montée, 15mm long, color A (mauve)

6 faceted ovals, 4mm dia., color A (mauve)

20 bicones, 4mm dia., color B (dark purple)

16 bicones, 4mm dia., color C (fuchsia)

11/0 rocailles, dark purple

56 in. (1.4m) beading thread

2 beading needles

Difficulty ★ ★ ★

Technique: Assembling Picks (See page 17.)

1 On the center of the thread, string one rocaille. Pass both threads through one bicone in color C to make the pick. On each thread, string one bicone in color B. Cross in one faceted oval. On the right thread (red), string one rocaille, one bicone in color B, one rocaille, one faceted oval, and one rocaille. Pass through the bottom right hole of the montée, and exit the top right hole. Add one rocaille. Cross through the faceted oval. String one rocaille, one bicone in color B, and one rocaille. Repeat with the left thread (blue). Cross in one faceted oval.

2 On each thread, string one bicone in color B. Cross the right thread (blue) through the bicone on the left thread. On the left thread (red), string one bicone in color C and one rocaille. Pass the thread back through the bicone in color C and the bicone in color B to make the pick.

3 | On the left thread (blue), string one bicone in color C, one rocaille, one bicone in color B, one rocaille, one faceted oval, one rocaille, and one bicone in color C. Pass the thread through the montée from the top hole to the bottom hole as shown. Thread one bicone in color C and one rocaille. Pass in the faceted oval. Add one rocaille, one bicone in color B, one rocaille, and one bicone in color C. Pass in one bicone. Repeat with the right thread (red).

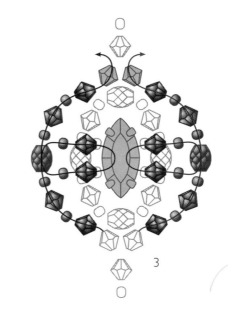

3

TIP

Hold the threads tight while you make the picks so that they are straight.

4 | Pass the right thread (red) through one bicone. Add one bicone in color C, one rocaille, and one bicone in color B. Pass through the montée. Add one bicone in color B, one rocaille, and one bicone in color C. Pass through the beads as shown.

4

5 | Pass the right thread (blue) to the right through the outside beads to the bottom left bicone. Add one bicone in color C, one rocaille, and one bicone in color B. Cross through the montée. Add one bicone in color B, one rocaille, and one bicone in color C. Pass through the beads. Cross in the left faceted oval. Refer to page 18 to make the band, beginning it as shown and continuing with the rocailles. End symmetrically. Join the threads, and knot them.

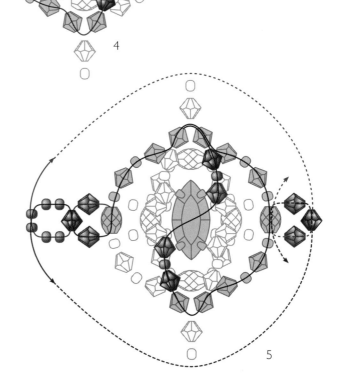

5

MIDNIGHT RING

Materials

24 faceted ovals, 4mm dia.,
color A (crystal)

12 bicones, 4mm dia., color B
(dark blue)

20 round beads, 4mm dia., color B
(dark blue)

11/0 rocailles, midnight blue

12 faceted ovals, crystal
(for ring band)

56 in. (1.4m) beading thread

2 beading needles

Difficulty ★ ★ ★

*Technique: The Square Cross
(See Page 20.)*

1   Use the faceted ovals to make a carpet of nine squares. Cross in the bottom right oval.

2   For the first flower, on the right thread (red), string one round, one rocaille, and one bicone. Cross in the top oval of the square. On the left thread (blue), string one round. Cross in one rocaille. Add one round. Cross in the top oval of the square. For the second flower, on the left thread (blue), string one bicone, one rocaille, and one round. Cross in the top oval of the square. Cross the right thread (red) through the round and one rocaille. Add one bicone. Cross in the top oval of the square. Make the third flower the same as the first, changing the position of the bicone. Cross in the top oval.

3   Move to the next column of the carpet, passing and crossing the threads as shown. (To do this, it may be easier to work on the wrong side.)

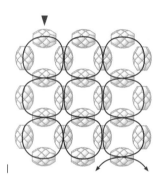

1

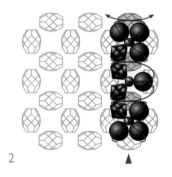

2

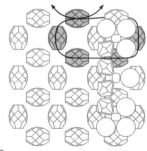

3

4 Follow the diagram to make the flowers on the second column. See step 3, and move to the next column of the carpet. Make the flowers on the third column. (Be sure to have the bicones on the inside of the assembly and the round beads on the outside.) Center the flower using all of the round beads. Cross through the top left faceted oval.

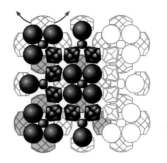

5 Pass the right thread (red) to the right and the left thread (blue) to the left through the faceted ovals, inserting one rocaille between the ovals. Cross in the corner rocaille. Cross each thread through one faceted oval.

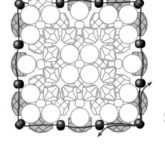

6 On each thread, string four rocailles. Cross in the corner rocaille. Pass in one rocaille. On each thread, string one rocaille. Cross in the faceted oval. Refer to page 18 to make the ring band, continuing it with the rocailles and faceted ovals. End symmetrically. Join the threads, and knot them.

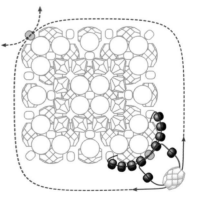

TIP
Create a variation by simply using other bead shapes and colors.

CONSTELLATION RING

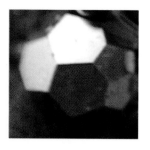

Materials

15 round beads, 6mm dia., color A (metallic gray)

20 bicones, 4mm dia., color B (light gray)

1 round bead, 8mm dia., color C (dark gray)

11/0 rocailles, metallic gray

12 faceted ovals, dark gray (for ring band)

60 in. (1.5m) beading thread

2 beading needles

Difficulty ★ ★ ★

Technique: The 5-Rose (See page 23.)

1 On the center of the thread, string four 6mm rounds. Cross in the bead at the right. On the outside thread (blue), string three 6mm rounds. Cross in the last bead strung. Repeat three times. Cross in the bead as shown.

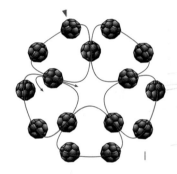

2 Work clockwise. On the left thread (blue), string one rocaille, one bicone, one rocaille, one bicone, and one rocaille. On the right thread (red), string one rocaille and one bicone. Cross in one rocaille. String one bicone and one rocaille. Cross in the round. Repeat four times.

2

3 On the right thread (red), string one rocaille, one 8mm round, and one rocaille. Pass in the beads to the left. Add one rocaille to every two beads. Pass the left thread (blue) to the right to cross in the beads. Begin the band as shown, continuing with the faceted ovals. End symmetrically. Join the threads, and knot them.

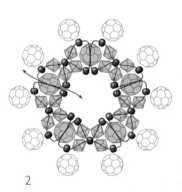
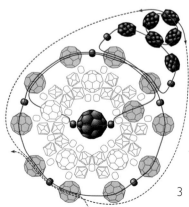

3

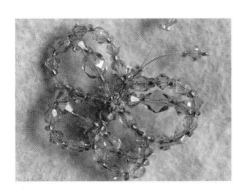

PIN

PENDANTS

BRACELETS